John's Logos

Daniel Amari

RRI publication

THE BACKGROUND OF LOGOS IN THE PROLOGUE OF JOHN

Dedication

This work would not have been possible if not for the prayers, encouragement and sacrifice of my wife, my parents, my family, my dean, my professors and the people of God. I thank the Lord for them. Soli Deo Gloria.

Table of Contents

Abbreviations

LXX	The Septuagint
NT	New Testament
OT	Old Testament
AD	Anno Domini
BC	Before Christ
BDAG	A Greek-English Lexicon of the New Testament and Other Early Christian Literature.
HALOT	Hebrew and Aramaic Lexicon of the Old Testament.
KJV	King James Version
NIV	New International Version
ESV	English Standard Version
NKJV	New King James Version
YNG	Young's Literal Translation
NLT	New Living Translation

Introduction

Defining Background

Everett Ferguson defines the concept of "parallels" which describes the "relation of Christianity to its context."[1] Parallels are similarities between Christianity and the religious, historical, geographical, and social context. According to Ferguson, a parallel does not necessarily imply that a concept in Christianity was derived from its parallel, nor does it necessarily imply that there is no such relationship.[2] In this book, a background of a text is defined as a parallel or set of parallels whose relationship to the text is concrete, in that the author of the text was familiar with the parallel, utilized it, and derived some of his concepts from it. The dependency of the text on the parallel cannot be explained away as a coincidence. Why only focus on those parallels that offer concrete relationship to the text? Because those parallels without such relationship are unhelpful in understanding the text. They are irrelevant to the text's origin and theology.

---

[1] Everett Ferguson, *Backgrounds of Early Christianity* (Grand Rapids: Eerdmans, 2003), 1.
[2] Ferguson, *Backgrounds of Early Christianity*, 2.

One would imagine that there are parallels that are relevant that have similarities but differ in the degree of similarities and relevance. For this book, these will be divided into two types of backgrounds: primary and secondary backgrounds. Then what is the methodology to differentiate between a primary and a secondary background? First, there must be a set of criteria within the context of the text itself that provides us with data for comparison. The original text offers a worldview, a concept, or an understanding. That worldview or concept is revealed from the exegesis of the text. The criteria encapsulate and summarize that worldview. These criteria will be enumerated later. They determine whether a candidate background is the right background for the concept. Moreover, a primary background fulfills the criteria for being the background of the concept. At a minimum, the primary background, if there is one, will fulfill some criteria and will not contradict others. A secondary background does not fulfill the criteria. It might fulfill some of the criteria, but it will contradict some of them. This is an important distinction between a primary and a secondary background, in that a secondary background will contradict some of the criteria. However, a secondary background can be useful in many instances. For example, John can indirectly contrast his idea with the idea from a secondary background. In other words, the secondary background does not help in positively defining and understanding the concept that John had in mind when writing his Prologue, but it can help in explaining what John is arguing against and contrasting. The goal of this book is to seek primary backgrounds.

Furthermore, one can pursue the background of the concept or the background of the term. The background of the concept focuses on the motif and the doctrines. The background of the term, λόγος (logos), focuses on the precise Greek term that was utilized. Ultimately, the goal is to find the background of the concepts found in the Prologue. At the same time, finding the background of the concept will probably direct us towards the background of the term. It is possible that the background of the concept and the background of the term are different; however, it is more probable that they will be the same. If a background of the concept is found and that background utilizes the term, then it is more suitable to specify the background of the term from the background of the concept. This is important because one cannot argue the opposite direction.

Next is the definition of a sub-background. A sub-background is a subset of a larger background in which the larger background contains diverse material that can be divided into smaller backgrounds. The smaller backgrounds can possibly still share common elements. They can possibly work together to create one larger background. The Old Testament background can be divided into smaller backgrounds, such as the Angel of the Lord, wisdom, creation, and others. All of these sub-backgrounds can be possibly considered as legitimate candidates for the background of the concept. This book will seek to show that the Old Testament is the exclusive primary background by demonstrating that either one of the sub-backgrounds is the primary background, or the Old Testament as a whole contains enough evidence to be the primary background. C. K. Barrett suggests that John's dependence on the Old Testament is not on a particular section but on the entire OT.[3]

---

[3] C. K. Barrett, *The Gospel According to St. John: An Introduction with Commentary and Notes on the Greek Text* (Philadelphia: The Westminster Press, 1978), 30.

Survey of Main Candidate Backgrounds

There are three main candidate backgrounds suggested by various scholars for the Prologue of John regarding the λόγος (logos). First, most if not all see the Old Testament as at least a primary background for this passage. This can be demonstrated through the direct quotations from the OT. The Gospel of John does not quote any other source. This fact raises the following question: Why would John not make at least one direct quotation from any other source if there were other sources as primary backgrounds? This argument is amplified when considering that in addition to direct quotations, many themes of the OT have been "woven into the structure of the Fourth Gospel without explicit citation of the OT," as Raymond Brown states.[4] In fact, Rudolph Schnackenburg asserts that the way John used the quotations proves that his knowledge of scripture is wide.[5]

Furthermore, Brown emphasizes that the dependence of the Gospel of John on the Old Testament is greater than the dependence of the synoptic Gospels on the Old Testament.[6] There is an established consensus or majority agreement on the direct dependence of John upon the Old Testament. Barrett asserts that John utilizes the Old Testament extensively, "This is seen most clearly in the extended allegories of the shepherd (10:1-16) and the vine (15:1-6)."[7] Gerald Borchert states that the Gospel of John "literally breathes the influence of Israel's

[4] Raymond E. Brown, *The Gospel According to John: Introduction, Translation, and Notes* (Garden City: Doubleday, 1966), LX.
[5] Rudolph Schnackenburg, *The Gospel According to St. John* (New York: Herder & Herder, 1968), 123.
[6] Brown, *The Gospel According to John*, LX.
[7] Barrett, *The Gospel According to St. John*, 30.

textbook."[8] Paul Hoskins asserts that John repeatedly presents Jesus as "the one who fulfills and replaces Old Testament institutions, events and themes that have anticipated him."[9] F.F. Bruce makes a similar claim, "the true background to John's thought and language is found not in Greek philosophy but in Hebrew revelation. The 'word of God" in the Old Testament denotes God in action, especially in creation, revelation and deliverance."[10] D.A. Carson summarizes the findings and the statements above:

> The fundamentally Jewish and Old Testament background to John's Gospel is increasingly recognized. What we call the Old Testament is what he repeatedly quotes, and that to which he repeatedly and explicitly alludes.[11]

The Chapters on the exegesis discusses about 30 distinct passages from the Old Testament to which the Prologue of John alludes, both directly and indirectly. There is no controversy here. Nevertheless, there are three concerns that need to be dealt with: First, some scholars suggest that the OT is not the only primary background. They suggest other backgrounds in additional to the OT. Third, some utilize limited OT material to link the prologue of John to the OT. Some scholars limit the definition of the OT background by only considering select verses from the OT or the LXX that contain the term λόγος (logos). For example, many refer to Isa 55:10-11. They see that

---

[8] Gerald Borchert, *An Exegetical and Theological Exposition of Holy Scripture* (Broadman & Holman Publishers, 1996), 61.
[9] Paul M. Hoskins, *Jesus as the Fulfillment of the Temple in the Gospel of John, Paternoster Biblical Monographs* (Milton Keynes: Paternoster, 2006) 123.
[10] F.F. Bruce, *The Gospel & Epistles of John* (Grand Rapids, Eerdmans, 1983), 29.
[11] D.A. Carson, *The Gospel According to John* (Eerdmans, 1991), 59.

---

the LXX usage of the λόγος (logos) portrays the word of God as "an active force or power going forth from him in fulfillment of His will and having results such as creation, renewal, inspiration."[12] Therefore, in general, when referring to the OT background, the classical approach is to refer only to those select verses and exclude the rest of the OT material, such as the wisdom of the OT, the names of God, the Angel of the Lord, the Christophany and Theophany appearances, and others. This excluded OT material has historically been incorporated with other backgrounds by scholars such as Brown[13] and James Dunn[14]. For example, the wisdom part of the OT (Proverbs) is included as part of the later wisdom literature background. Despite the fact that the OT background is limited to those select verses that contain the term λόγος, there is no denial that OT is still seen as a primary background. William Hendriksen suggests that this is how we should understand the meaning of the λόγος in that "Christ is the Word of God in both respects: he expresses or reflects the mind of God; also, he reveals God to man."[15] When some scholars, including Brown, dismiss the Old Testament background as the exclusive primary one, they do so based only on a few selected verses . They argue that the Isaiah quotation is not a sufficient passage in the Old Testament because it does not personify the λόγος and does not portray him as a person with eternal fellowship with God. Furthermore, these

---

[12] R.H. Lightfoot, *St. John's Gospel: A Commentary* (London: Oxford University Press, 1956), 52.
[13] Brown, *The Gospel According to John,* 521-522.
[14] James Dunn, *Christology in the Making: A New Testament Inquiry into the Origins of the Doctrine of Incarnation* (Philadelphia: Westminster Press, 1980), 218-219.
[15] William Hendriksen, *New Testament Commentary: John Volume 1* (Grand Rapids: Baker, 1953), 70.

passages, such as the one in Isaiah, can be explained as a metaphor for the act and the power of God. 'Metaphor' falls short of a direct reference to the concept of the eternal person of the Son who was in eternal relationship with the Father. The λόγος references in the Old Testament can explain the choice of λόγος in John. But these references cannot explain the full concept articulated by the Prologue of John. The goal of this book is to demonstrate that the Old Testament is not merely a primary background but the only exclusive primary background. One of the ways in which this goal will be achieved is through exploring wider material from each of the three backgrounds.

The second background is the writings of Philo. The Philo background contains many elements that make it worthy to be examined in detail. The λόγος in Philo is strongly used as a personified entity that is connected back to the Old Testament. Philo examines the various passages in the Old Testament and attributes them to an entity called the λόγος. This background might seem to be the missing link. But why was this background not adopted by the overwhelming majority of scholars, such as Borchert [16], Brown [17], Carson [18], C. H. Dodd [19], Stephen Smalley[20], B. F. Westcott[21] and Schnackenburg[22]. There are strong objections against this background. 1. The λόγος in

---

[16] Gerald Borchert, *An Exegetical and Theological Exposition of Holy Scripture* (Broadman & Holman Publishers, 1996), 74.
[17] Brown, *The Gospel According to John*, LVIII.
[18] Carson, *The Gospel According to John*, 115.
[19] C.H. Dodd, *The interpretation of the Fourth Gospel* (Cambridge University Press, 1954),73.
[20] Stephen S. Smalley, *John Evangelist & Interpreter* (Downers Grove: InterVarsity Press, 1998), 64.
[21] B. F. Westcott, *The Gospel According to St. John: The Authorized Version with Introduction and Notes* (Grand Rapids: Eerdmans, 1971), xvi.
[22] Schnackenburg, *The Gospel According to St. John*, 125.

Philo's writings is a created entity; in John the λόγος is not created. 2. In Philo the λόγος is impersonal; in John, the λόγος is personal. 3. In the words of Hendriksen, Philo's writings cannot be considered as a background due to the excessive unsystematic allegorizing that Philo employed. His thinking takes its concepts to a wide range of domains so that "the term as employed by the evangelist cannot derive its meaning from such allegorization."[23] Philo's concept stands in contrast to the precise, clear concept found in the Prologue of John. An overwhelming majority of scholars see Greek philosophies, such as Platonism, to be the heart of the concept of the λόγος in Philo's writings. These include Harry Wolfson[24], David Runia[25], C. K. Barrett[26], and B. F. Westcott[27]. As will be demonstrated later, these Platonic concepts behind the λόγος of Philo are in contrast to the concepts of the Prologue. Larry Hurtado states:

> The prologue is the Johannine passage that often has been thought to offer the strongest possibilities for a connection to Philo. But even here, beyond the coincidental (and very different) use of 'Logos' by both authors, there is in fact nothing specific for which Philo is essential to understand it.[28]

[23] Hendriksen, *New Testament Commentary*, 69.

[24] Harry Austryn Wolfson, *Philo: Foundations of Religious Philosophy in Judaism, Christianity, and Islam* (Cambridge: Harvard University Press, 1962), 95.

[25] David T. Runia, "Philo of Alexandria," in *Routledge Encyclopedia of Philosophy*, ed. Edward Craig (New York: Routledge, 1998), 358.

[26] Barrett, *The New Testament Background*, 262.

[27] Westcott, *The Gospel According to St. John*, XVII.

[28] Larry W. Hurtado, "Does Philo Help Explain Early Christianity," in *Philo und das Neue Testament*, ed. Roland Deines and Karl-Wilhelm Niebuhr (Tübingen: Mohr Siebeck, 2004), 78.

It seems that scholarship has moved from Philo to other backgrounds. Even if this is the case, the insight from investigating Philo's writings is extremely valuable. Furthermore, in recent years, there has been a resurrection of this background by some scholars, such as James Dunn[29] and Elizabeth Harris[30].

The third background is the wisdom literature. Lightfoot suggests that this can be a suitable background; he adds, "In Proverbs 8:22-31 Wisdom is said to have been possessed or formed by Yahweh before all things, and to have been His counselor and architect in the creation of the universe."[31] Almost always when speaking of the wisdom background, scholars see the OT wisdom component and the wisdom literature of the second-temple era as one and the same. This could be attributed to the influence of select prominent scholars, such as Brown. However, many scholars, such as Carson[32], Hurtado,[33] and Harris[34] rightly question whether this is the primary background. For example, if John wanted to refer to wisdom, why didn't he use σοφία instead of λόγος? Despite the fascinating parallelism between λόγος and Wisdom, one must ask why only use λόγος? As Carson states:

---

[29] Dunn, *Christology in the Making*, 221-227.
[30] Elizabeth Harris, *Prologue and Gospel. The Theology of the Fourth Evangelist*, JSNTSup 107 (Sheffield: Sheffield Academic Press, 1995), 201.
[31] Lightfoot, *St. John's Gospel,* 54.
[32] Carson, *The Gospel According to John,* 116.
[33] Hurtado, *Lord Jesus Christ,* 366.
[34] Harris, *Prologue and Gospel. The Theology of the Fourth Evangelist,* 198.

The lack of Wisdom terminology in John's Gospel suggests that the parallels between Wisdom and John's λόγος may stem less from direct dependence than from common dependence on Old Testament.[35]

In other words, where is the link between the wisdom writings and the Prologue of John? For this reason, some scholars, such as T. H. Tobin[36], have branched out to include Philo's writings as a linguistic connector between John and the wisdom writings.

The Five Parameters

When considering the background of the λόγος of John, there are several points to note:

First, Hurtado warns against "simplistic notions of influence" when it comes to investigating backgrounds. He adds that healthy religious systems redefine their terms, and therefore any system should not be adopted as a background based on a shared term.[37] The fact that John carefully defines the λόγος in his Prologue suggests that his intention is not to refer to a concept or another term that utilizes the λόγος, nor is to appeal to another group of people who have certain affinity for that term. Instead, it is about defining and communicating the concept. Therefore, a candidate background of the term cannot be used to override or redefine the usage of the λόγος in the Gospel of John. For example, one cannot force Philo's philosophical views and his LXX interpretation on the Prologue

---

[35] Carson, *The Gospel According to John*, 115.

[36] T.H. Tobin, "The Prologue of John and Hellenistic Jewish Speculation," *CBQ* 52 (1990): 256.

[37] Larry Hurtado, *Lord Jesus Christ* (Grand Rapids: Eerdmans, 2003) 366.

of John, just because John uses the term λόγος. Moreover, the principle stands true even if it is found that Philo's writings were the primary reason for the widespread use of λόγος in the first century and eventually for the adoption of it in the Gospel of John.

Second, the richness of the λόγος background, in that it is used in a wide spectrum of religious and philosophical writings, suggests that careful consideration should be taken before adopting a particular background. The richness of the background is demonstrated by the over-utilization of the term λόγος as both the literal everyday usage and as the term that encapsulates a philosophical or theological thought. The richness is demonstrated and amplified as more recent discoveries are being made, which provide us with better information to evaluate the relevant background. This might suggest, as Carson puts it:

> The wealth of possible backgrounds to the term λόγος in John's prologue suggests that the determining factor is not this or that background but the church's experience of Jesus Christ.[38]

Third, the term λόγος was utilized only two times in the Gospel of John to refer to Christ. Therefore, the lack of utilization of the term λόγος suggests that the literal term is not the overriding theological principle in the Gospel of John. Otherwise, John would have used it to describe Christ in every opportunity. It further suggests that the term itself cannot be the criteria for finding the background. In other words, finding another religious or philosophical system that utilizes the term

---

[38] Carson, *The Gospel According to John*, 116.

λόγος does not automatically mean that this is the background. It is possible and probable that John heard a certain term utilized in a certain context, whether it was linguistic, religious, historical, or philosophical. Then he borrowed that term and redefined it as he saw fit for his Gospel. The act of borrowing against a certain context does not automatically qualify that context to be the primary background. The reason for this is that diverse philosophical and religious systems share many common terms. That does not mean they are related.

Fourth, the exegesis of the Prologue is the overriding factor for understanding and tracing back to the source background. This is accomplished by identifying the parameters within the Prologue that will point back to the backgrounds for the λόγος. Here is the reason why: John utilizes the term λόγος in the most specific, accurate, and targeted way possible. John uses the term λόγος in the context of 18 verses with the following five parameters: The λόγος is eternal, personal, God, creator, and has become flesh. The background of the λόγος will not answer any supposed ambiguity about the basic elements of John's Prologue. The primary background will not answer questions about whether or not the λόγος is God, or whether or not the λόγος was created. John already provides these answers. They constitute the parameters with which we evaluate whether a candidate background is a primary background or not. What about a scenario where John borrowed a system and modified it? Wouldn't that original system be considered a primary background? The answer for this scenario depends on how much John modified the original system. If the original system was modified completely, then it only contributed the term. In this case, it cannot be a primary background because it does not fit the criteria. If the original system was only slightly modified to the extent that its concepts fulfill the criteria or at least do not contradict any of them, then it can be considered a primary background. The point is that there are in reality two systems for this scenario: original and modified. We are evaluating the original for what it is; any modified system is a new system even if it borrowed the main term from an original one. Furthermore, these criteria can help us locate the closest candidate background from which John possibly borrowed and derived his own concept. It is more reasonable to assume that John would utilize a closer system for modification and derivation than a further system. Moreover, there needs to be concrete evidence, such as direct quotations, that demonstrates that John borrowed from the original background and then modified it for his purposes. This principle of requiring a candidate background to adhere to the parameters that are clearly found in the Prologue of John is not an arbitrary assertion of this book. This principle is a common theme accepted by scholars, such as Gunter Reim[39] and George Ladd.[40]

The five parameters, mentioned in the previous paragraph, will be demonstrated above in the next chapters. Since John's Prologue provides these parameters about the λόγος, one should expect that the primary background would provide the same parameters. At a minimum, if it provides some, it should not contradict the rest of the parameters. If one requires further clarification to the meaning of the Prologue, then the rest of the Gospel of John provides more demonstration and examples for further understanding. The background provides depth and

[39] Gunter Reim, "Jesus as God in the Fourth Gospel: The Old Testament Background," *NTS* 30 (1984): 158–159.
[40] George Eldon Ladd, *A Theology of the New Testament* (Grand Rapids: Eerdmans, 1993) 277-278.

dimension, not contradicting elements. Looking for traces of these elements in various backgrounds is the most important guiding principle that this book will follow. The agreement of the candidate background with the concepts in the Prologue demonstrates that the candidate background is the primary one. This principle is more appropriate than the assumption that John's Prologue was an evolution based on a background that offered contradictory concepts. One cannot seriously consider a background that contradicted the elements that are in the Prologue. For example, to those who advocate Gnostic or Hellenistic backgrounds, Brown follows Dodd and says, "No Hellenistic thinker would see a climax in the Incarnation, just as no Gnostic would triumphantly proclaim that the Word had become flesh."[41] When considering a background, one must look for the background that agrees with the foundational elements of the Prologue of John.

---

[41] Brown, *The Gospel According to John*, 25.

Exegesis

The Prologue of John

The Prologue cannot be separated from the rest of the Gospel of John. The Prologue and the Gospel are unified and depend on each other, and are the same literary work. At the same time, it is not possible to arrive at different conclusions even if the exegesis of the Prologue is done outside the context of the rest of the Gospel. This is not an invitation for an isolated exegesis of the Prologue of John. It is an acceptance of the reality that the rest of the Gospel amplifies and expands upon certain parameters of the Prologue. Why should one exclude the rest of the Gospel when it provides the material that further clarifies the intention of the author?

Furthermore, it will be demonstrated, as the result of the exegesis of the Prologue, that the author of this Gospel has not been restricted by only utilizing the LXX. Barrett provides a very remarkable statement, "this brief analysis suggests, as has been said, that John regularly used the LXX, but that he was able to use, and on occasion did use, the Hebrew." [42] These chapters will show that John was not limited by the LXX and when he wanted to use the Hebrew, he had no problem using it. When there was a relevant difference between both texts, he selected the appropriate one. Furthermore, there is the suggestion that John expected his audience to have a deep familiarity with the

---

[42] Barrett, *The Gospel According to St. John*, 29.

Old Testament, the kind of familiarity that transcends one language or one translation. This conclusion can only be supported after careful exegesis of the Prologue. This type of argument requires passing over the same text multiple times. This is the reason that the Hebrew text is compared to the LXX text.

Finally, it should not be surprising that the exegesis undertaken here will show the dependency of John on the OT. This is unavoidable because the Gospel of John directly quotes from the OT and repeatedly alludes to it.

In the beginning (εν ἀρχῇ)

The Gospel of John begins with the existence of the λόγος. In particular, it is not whether the λόγος exists or not, but the manner of existence. John 1:1a states Εν ἀρχῇ ἦν ὁ λόγος (En archē ēn ho logos, in the beginning was the word). To what does the ἀρχῇ (archē, beginning) refer? What origin does it give to the λόγος? The answer proposed most often is Gen 1:1, because the first phrase of the books of Genesis and John is Εν ἀρχῇ (En archē). However, before any possible relationship between Genesis and John 1:1 is sought, the intended meaning of John 1:1a must be established from the context of the Prologue and the Gospel of John. In order to understand the relationship between ἀρχῇ (archē) of John 1:1a and the λόγος, ἦν (ēn, was) needs to be understood. The value of ἦν (ēn) takes on additional weight and specificity within the Prologue of John due to a pattern that is formed by the author. In particular, the pattern is established when ἦν (ēn) is contrasted with ἐγένετο (egeneto, became) throughout the Prologue. Such a pattern indicates that the author has written the Prologue with a certain level of precision and care. When John wanted to convey, in the Prologue, that an entity or an event began in a point of time, he utilized the verb ἐγένετο (egeneto). This is seen in verses 3 and 10 when describing the beginning of creation. It is used in verse 6 when talking about John the Baptist. It is also used in verse 12 to describe how humans become children of God, and in verse

14 to describe the incarnation. It is used in verse 15 to describe how Jesus surpasses John the Baptist. In verse 17, it is used to describe the new dispensation of the grace and truth of Jesus. All the references in the Gospel of John that utilize any form of the verb γίνομαι were examined. Every one of the more than 50 instances communicates the idea of beginning at a certain point of time. On the other hand, ἦν might not have the distinct opposite meaning, for there are instances in the Gospel of John in which it is used as ἐγένετο (egeneto). However, in contrast to ἐγένετο, especially in the context of the Prologue and the context of other specific passages of the Gospel, it portrays a process in the past and not a beginning at a certain point. This might be magnified by the fact that it is in the imperfect tense which conveys the imperfective aspect and a sense of temporal remoteness. This provides a distinctive meaning to John 1:1a. Barrett states that the contrast between h=n and ἐγένετο, "indicates that by ἀρχή (archē) is meant not the first point in temporal sequences but that which lies beyond time."[43] If the beginning of the creation of everything is what is intended by ἀρχή, then the λόγος was already in existence. However, John 1:1a states more than just that the λόγος was already in existence during creation. For the statement of John 1:1a is absolute, and thus it requires a meaningful declaration that better identifies the manner of the existence of the λόγος. If the comparison is to ἐγένετο, then the meaning of h=n cannot contain a beginning. There is no beginning point in which the λόγος did not exist. In short, what John 1:1a communicates is that the λόγος is eternal. Carson suggests another example in the Gospel of John that

---

[43] Barrett, *The Gospel According to St. John*, 152.

contrasts εἰμί (eimi, am) with γίνομαι (ginomai, become).[44] In John 8:58, Jesus states, πρὶν Ἀβραὰμ γενέσθαι ἐγὼ εἰμι (prin Abraam genesthai egō eimi, before Abraham became I AM). There is more than just the existence of Jesus before Abraham. There is eternity. The perfective aspect (which shows complete action) of the aorist verb γενέσθαι (genesthai, became) on the imperfective aspect (which suggests continuous process) of the present verb εἰμι (eimi, am), combined with the contrast between εἰμί with γίνομαι suggest that Jesus eternally existed and always existed. This is compared to the limited span of Abraham in which his existence is portrayed as complete and finite. There is more to this verse than eternal existence and there is more evidence to collaborate the eternity of Jesus in John 8:58.

In light of the fact that John 1:1a indicates the eternity of the λόγος, is there a relationship to Genesis 1? Craig Evans suggests, "The conceptual parallels are obvious and quite significant."[45] In particular, the parallels come from creation where God created light and gave life. However, Rudolph Bultmann claims that John 1:1 cannot be linked to Genesis 1 because Gen 1:1 communicates a temporal event while John 1:1 communicates an eternal being.[46] Bultmann's assertion that John's λόγος is eternal is valid. However, there is a way to link John 1:1 with Gen 1:1 without violating the eternity of the λόγος. If John 1:1a is to be compared to Genesis 1, then the common point between the two clauses is not that God created the λόγος in the beginning, as he created the heavens and earth. Rather, the λόγος

---

[44] Carson, *The Gospel According to John*, 114.
[45] Craig A. Evans, *Word and Glory: On the Exegetical and Theological Background of John's Prologue* (Sheffield Academic press, 1993), 78.
[46] Rudolf Bultmann, *The Gospel of John: A Commentary* (Westminster Press, 1971), 21.

of John is God the creator in Genesis. Since God, in Gen 1:1, was there during the act of creation but outside the domain of creation, the λόγος was outside of the domain of creation and existed before any act of creation occurred. In other words, both God and the λόγος were not created. Furthermore, even if Genesis 1 is not a connection to John 1:1, that should not exclude the rest of the OT. Many religious and philosophical systems build bridges to Gen 1:1. That fact is not enough connection to the Prologue of John. The important thing is how they build the bridge and how they portray their own primary entity. Many systems, such as those found in Philo or wisdom literature, place their entities at Gen 1:1 while asserting that the λόγος was created before that. It is insufficient that a certain system portrays its λόγος as created before everything. As Schnackenburg states, "The Logos was not created, he simply 'was', that is, he already existed, absolutely, timeless and eternal."[47]

There are several OT passages that may serve as the background for the timeless and eternal nature of the λόγος. The first reference is Isa 43:13. This is an important verse because Carson suggests Isa 43:13 as a verse that contains a parallel to John 8:58 in which Jesus identifies himself with the Lord.[48] This verse can be explored as a starting point for a possible connection to John 1:1a. In particular, is eternity communicated in Isa 43:13? The verse states גַּם־מִיּוֹם אֲנִי הוּא (ma-mīyōm ʾănī hū). Typically, the verse is translated "from ancient days, I am he; or from that day or today, I am he." The LXX does not translate אֲנִי הוּא (ʾănī hū, I am he). Therefore, if absolute

---

[47] Schnackenburg, *The Gospel According to St. John*, 232.
[48] Carson, *The Gospel According to John*, 358.

dependence of John on the LXX is assumed, the connection from John 8:58 to Isa 43:13 cannot be easily established. Therefore, the path to this verse has to be a different one from the LXX. As it will be demonstrated later, the connection of John to the Hebrew text goes deeper than is apparent.

The second verse to be considered is Deut 33:27. In searching for verses that describe God as eternal, Deut 33:27 is a good starting point. In it, God is described as eternal: אֱלֹהֵי קֶדֶם ('ĕlōhē qeḏem, eternal God). The LXX translates masculine קֶדֶם (qeḏem) with feminine ἀρχῆς associating it with another feminine noun. Despite this different association, קֶדֶם (qeḏem) can be a starting point for searching the Hebrew text. All references of קֶדֶם (qeḏem) in the Old Testament have been examined. The word has several meanings. It mostly means 'east' or 'ancient.' It is used as a preposition and as a verb in several instances. But there are only a few instances in which it means eternal. For example, Psa 74:12 states וֵאלֹהִים מַלְכִּי מִקֶּדֶם (wēlōhīm malkī miqqeḏem, and God is my king from eternity). The LXX translates it as ὁ δὲ θεὸς βασιλεὺς ἡμῶν πρὸ αἰῶνος (ho de theos basileus hēmōn pro aiōnos). This leads to Mic 5:2 which states מִקֶּדֶם מִימֵי עוֹלָם (miqqeḏem mīmē 'ōlām, from ancient from the days of eternity); and thus, associates קֶדֶם (qeḏem) with עוֹלָם ('ōlām, eternity), the latter meaning 'eternity.' The LXX translates it as follows: ἀπ' ἀρχῆς ἐξ ἡμερῶν αἰῶνος (ap' archēs ex hēmerōn aiōnos). Mic 5:2 is a prophecy about the Messiah in which it describes him as eternal. Hab 1:12 (NLT) states the following: O Lord my God…you who are eternal(מִקֶּדֶם, miqqeḏem). The LXX translates מִקֶּדֶם (miqqeḏem) as ἀπ' ἀρχῆς. There is a Hebrew term that is associated with ἀρχῇ, namely רֹאשׁ (rōš, head/beginning). Several passages in Isaiah contain רֹאשׁ (rōš) and their corresponding LXX translations contain ἀρχῇ, such as Isa 41:4 and Isa 48:16. However, there is another unique verse, Pro 8:23, that probably provides one of the best connections to John 1:1a. Pro 8:23 states: From eternity (מֵעוֹלָם, mēʿōlām, from eternity) I was appointed from the beginning (מֵרֹאשׁ, mērōš). While the LXX renders רֹאשׁ (rōš) as ἀρχῇ, רֹאשׁ (rōš) is associated with עוֹלָם (ʿōlām).

With God (πρὸς τὸν θεόν)

John 1:1b states, and the Word was with God. The λόγος is not the same person referred to by τὸν θεόν (ton theon) in John 1:1b. The phrase τὸν θεόν refers to the Father. If the λόγος was eternally with God and yet he is a distinct person from God, this leaves us with two possibilities; he is either a different God or a distinct person of the same God. Evidently, John takes his own Jewish monotheism for granted. Furthermore, he takes his reader's monotheism for granted as well. Later in many passages, John affirms the unity of the Father and the Son. In John 10:30, Jesus said, ἐγὼ καὶ ὁ πατὴρ ἕν ἐσμεν (egō kai ho patēr hen esmen, I and the Father are one). There is unity between the Father and the Son. They are the same monotheistic God, though they are distinct persons. The careful wording of John 1:1 and especially in 1:1c ensures that both unity in essence and distinction in personhood are not violated. Concerning the πρός (pros) in John 1:1b, there are 100 instances in the Gospel of John other than the two references in verses 1 and 2. Ninety-two percent of the instances have the meaning of 'towards' or 'to.' Sixty-one percent of the instances are associated with verbs such as ἔρχομαι (erchomai), ἀπέρχομαι (aperchomai), and πορεύω (poreuō). Thirty-one percent of the instances are associated with verbs such as λέγω (legō). The remaining eight percent include two instances with the meaning 'for' indicating 'purpose;' one instance with the meaning 'for' utilized to indicate 'time;' four dative instances conveying 'at' that indicate 'location' and one instance that conveys 'against.' None of them matches the meaning of the two instances in John 1:1b and John 1:2. There are several hypotheses that attempt to offer a solution for this. The first hypothesis is that John was not limited by his usages in his Gospel. There are instances in the New Testament that communicate the meaning 'with' in select verses, such as Matt 13:56 and Mark 14:49. In these instances, intimate personal relationship is not communicated, at least not clearly. There is an objection to this hypothesis. The Gospel of John contains an abundance of μετά (meta) and παρά (para) that means 'with' in a wide spectrum from an impersonal location to a very personal relationship between the Father and the Son. For example, John 8:29 states the following: καὶ ὁ πέμψας με μετ᾽ ἐμοῦ ἐστιν (kai ho pempsas me met᾽ emou estin, and the one who sent me is with me). John could have used either μετά or παρά in John 1:1b and 1:2. However, the fact that he utilized πρός raises the question whether there is a deliberate intention. This is not only true for the Gospel of John but for the rest of the Johannine literature with the exception of one reference: 1 John 1:2. However, that reference of the Prologue of 1 John is not helpful in solving the puzzle and does not break the statistics. It is possible to argue that the Prologue of 1 John is expected to contain such parallelism for it rehashes some of the ideas of the Prologue of John.

This brings us to the second hypothesis. Some suggest that the use of πρός instead of the default prepositions indicates a specific meaning intended by the author. In particular, it indicates the intimate personal relationship between the Father and the Son. This is because the usage of the preposition with an accusative noun indicates "a marker of movement of orientation towards someone or something."[49] Stanley Porter states that 'with' does not give full justice to the intended meaning of "face-to-face presence."[50] James White asserts that John conveys an idea similar to the one found in 1 Cor 13:12, πρόσωπον πρὸς πρόσωπον (prosōpon pros prosōpon) which conveys personal relationship. [51] However, 1 Cor 13:12 communicates an intimate personal relationship primarily because of the context and not because of the use of the preposition alone. The author examined all occurrences of πρός in the New Testament. There are three observations to be made. 1. Although the occurrence in 1 Cor 13:12 is probably not as strong by itself, 2 John 1:2b and 3 John 1:14 strengthen that theory. In other words, it is possible that πρός communicates personal relationship under certain contexts and conditions. 2. While it might be true that in general, the force of a transitive preposition is overridden by a stative verb, there might be a room for an exception when the proposition is πρός. No conclusive evidence was found to collaborate that rule. 3. Most importantly, all references of πρός in which a copulative verb associates an entity with a person, where the meaning of πρός is 'with,' that entity is a person with a personal knowledge of the other person. Carson suggests that "pros may mean 'with' only when a person is with a person, usually in some fairly intimate relationship."[52] In other words, even if the preposition's transitive force cannot be used conclusively to imply personal relationship, the

---

[49] *BDAG,* s.v. "πρὸς."
[50] Stanley E. Porter, *Idioms of the Greek New Testament* (England: Sheffield Academic Press, 1999), 173.
[51] James R. White, *The Forgotten Trinity: Recovering the Heart of Christian Belief* (Minneapolis: Bethany House Publishers, 1998), 52.
[52] Carson, *The Gospel According to John,* 116.

observed New Testament pattern of πρός suggests that the λόγος is a person. This seems to be the best explanation for the preposition. This conclusion is justified further, when the larger context is taken into consideration. In conclusion, πρός suggests one safe inference: the λόγος is a person. This eliminates the idea that the λόγος only became a person in the incarnation.

Beyond that, does this clause communicate anything else? The same verb ἦν (ēn) is utilized in this clause as well as John 1:1c. The pattern that John develops in contrasting ἦν with ἐγένετο (egeneto) suggests no point of beginning in the second clause. If ἐγένετο is utilized by John to indicate a beginning in time, then in contrast, ἦν is utilized to show existence or action that had no beginning. The same can be said of John 1:1c. There was no point of time in which the λόγος was not with the Father. This raises an important question: What have the two persons of the Godhead been doing beside each other since eternity? The simple reading of the passage suggests a subtlety of eternal purpose based on communion. It is an expectation of the author's introduction of the λόγος: If 1:1a speaks of the manner of existence and 1:1c speaks of his essence, as will be shown later, 1:1b is about the eternal purpose: What was the λόγος doing since eternity? The eternal purpose is the loving relationship with the Father. This has been stated by other scholars, communicated in the rest of the Prologue, and demonstrated in the rest of the Gospel.

First, there is scholarship support for this: Schnackenburg observes that the first verse reflects some sort of personal communion or "closeness" based on love between the λόγος and God.[53] Westcott, in his comments on John 1:1b, states:

---

[53] Schnackenburg, *The Gospel According to St. John*, 234.

The idea conveyed by it is not that of a simple coexistence as of two persons contemplated separately in a company... or united under common conception... or (so to speak) in local relation but of being (in some sense) directed towards and regulated by that with which the relationship is fixed. The personal being of the Word was realized in active intercourse with and in perfect communion with God.[54]

Second, the personhood of the λόγος and the personal relationship with the Father is not entirely based on John 1:1b. The Prologue of John suggests this as well. This will be demonstrated later in the exegesis of verses 14 and 18. Third, the rest of the Gospel provides many examples that solidify this point. In John 17:24, Jesus speaks to the Father about his glory that was given to him by the Father because "you loved me before the foundation of the world." This is connected to 17:5 about the restoration of Jesus' glory that he had before the world existed. It is not that the Father loved the Son from eternity, but that the Father loved the Son while the Son was there with him.

---

[54] Westcott, *The Gospel According to St. John*, 3.

God (θεός)

John 1:1c states that the λόγος is God: καὶ θεὸς ἦν ὁ λόγος (kai theos ēn ho logos). From a grammatical perspective, this is a predicate nominative construction in which the Greek article ὁ specifies the subject, namely λόγος, and the anarthrous θεός (theos) is the predicate.[55] If θεός is articular in this clause, then John "would have been so identifying the Word with God that no divine being could exist apart from the Word." [56] Furthermore, if θεός is articular, as in καὶ ὁ λόγος ἦν ὁ θεός, it can lead to a logical contradiction in the context of the whole verse in which the extra article, in its anaphoric usage, can point to the θεός in John 1:1b. This will imply that the λόγος was with God the Father and the λόγος was God the Father. The combination of the context of John 1:1b, the fact that the θεός is not the subject, and that the θεός is anarthrous, removes the possibility that this passage is communicating Modalism or Sabellianism. In fact, Daniel Wallace states that "the Fourth Gospel is about the least likely place to find modalism in the NT."[57] The λόγος is θεός without being the Father. What is the effect of the predicate nominative θεός preceding the λόγος? The effect is the emphasis of θεός.[58] Furthermore, the predicate

---

[55] Nigel Turner, *Syntax, vol. 3 of A Grammar of New Testament Greek* by J. H. Moulton (Edinburgh: T&T Clark, 1963), 183.
[56] Carson, *The Gospel According to John,* 117.
[57] Wallace, *Greek Grammar beyond the Basics*, 268.
[58] Carson, *The Gospel According to John,* 117.

nominative noun preceding the copulative verb has led to much debate about its nature: whether the predicate nominative noun is qualitative, definite, or indefinite. Colwell's Rule states that definite predicate nominative nouns that precede the copulative verb 'usually' do not need the Greek article when the context shows that the noun is definite.[59] Many have suggested that Colwell's Rule can apply to John 1:1c with the result that θεός is definite. For example, Porter stated that the translation 'and the word was God' is "a legitimate translation of the passage according to Colwell's work, if the predicate is definite."[60] The real question is: does this rule apply to John 1:1c? According to Colwell's Rule, he includes "only definite nouns among his anarthrous predicates."[61] This means that this rule requires a predetermination that the noun in question is definite, in order for the rule to be useful.[62] Wallace states that the rule does not imply that all anarthrous predicate nominative nouns which precede the copula are, or usually are, definite nouns.[63] Carson states the same: that one cannot make the case that an anarthrous predicate nominative noun preceding a copulative verb is "highly likely" definite based on that construction alone.[64] In other words, in order to determine whether the rule applies, other indicators such as context need to be utilized to determine if the predicate noun is definite.

---

[59] Wallace, *Greek Grammar beyond the Basics*, 257.
[60] Porter, *Idioms of the Greek New Testament*, 110.
[61] Turner, *Syntax, vol. 3 of A Grammar of New Testament Greek*, 184.
[62] Porter, *Idioms of the Greek New Testament*, 109.
[63] Wallace, *Greek Grammar beyond the Basics*, 257.
[64] D. A. Carson, *Exegetical Fallacies* (Grand Rapids: Baker Books, 1996), 84.

Wallace suggests that the predicate noun in John 1:1c is a qualitative one.[65] He provides the following evidence. He cites Phillip B. Harner's study in which Harner claims, "80% of Colwell's constructions involved qualitative nouns and only 20% involved definite nouns."[66] He also cites another study by Paul Stephen Dixon in which 94% of such constructions in John are qualitative nouns and only 6% are definite.[67] Wallace draws the following conclusion, "An anarthrous pre-verbal predicate nominative is normally qualitative, sometimes definite, and only rarely indefinite."[68] Furthermore, he suggests that the burden of proof is on the definite camp, and even more on the indefinite camp, to show that the noun is definite or indefinite.[69] Carson cites another study in which the distribution of pre-verbal predicate nominative nouns in the New Testament is equal between definite and indefinite ones.[70] Probably, in that study, the indefinite nouns included the qualitative ones. Even with the statistics cited by Wallace, it is possible that the predicate in John 1:1c is definite. Wallace cites John 1:49 as an example for a definite pre-verbal predicate nominative noun in which Nathaniel's response could only make sense if βασιλεὺς in σὺ βασιλεὺς εἶ τοῦ Ἰσραήλ (basileus in sy basileus ei tou Israēl) is definite.[71] Carson cites the same example as evidence that John used a definite predicate noun in the same chapter of John 1:1c.[72] The point is that Colwell's Rule shows that it is possible, when

---

[65] Wallace, *Greek Grammar beyond the Basics*, 269.
[66] Wallace, *Greek Grammar beyond the Basics*, 259.
[67] Wallace, *Greek Grammar beyond the Basics*, 260.
[68] Wallace, *Greek Grammar beyond the Basics*, 262.
[69] Wallace, *Greek Grammar beyond the Basics*, 263.
[70] Carson, *Exegetical Fallacies*, 84.
[71] Wallace, *Greek Grammar beyond the Basics*, 263.
[72] Carson, *The Gospel According to John*, 117.

appropriate, that an anarthrous pre-verbal predicate nominative noun is a definite one. Contextual evidence must show whether it is or it is not. The only non-grammatical objection that Wallace provides against the case of θεός being definite is the following: "Calling θεός in 1:1c definite is the same as saying that if it had followed the verb it would have had the article."[73] Thus, it would make the λόγος to be the Father. However, it is not convincing that a definite θεός in καὶ θεὸς ἦν ὁ λόγος is the same as καὶ ὁ λόγος ἦν ὁ θεός . The reason for this is that when θεός is articular, the Greek article can also assume an anaphoric function linking the Father with the Son. But in its current order, a definite anarthrous θεός does not have the anaphoric quality because it does not have the article. For John 1:1c, there are two factors that determine the precise meaning. The first factor is the order, as C. F. D. Moule suggests:

> It needs to be recognized that the Fourth Evangelist need not have chosen this word-order, and that his choice of it, though creating some ambiguity, may in itself be an indication of his meaning.[74]

The second factor is the selective use of the Greek article.

Moreover, Carson states that John 1:1c is communicating the identity of the λόγος and that does not have to contradict 1:1b, "for statements of identity are not necessarily reciprocal." [75] In other words, a definite θεός in 1:1c communicates the identity of the λόγος as θεός and not just his essence; stating that the identity of λόγος is θεός does not imply

---

[73] Wallace, *Greek Grammar beyond the Basics*, 268.
[74] C. F. D. Moule, *An Idiom Book of New Testament Greek* (Cambridge: Cambridge University Press, 1959), 116.
[75] Carson, *Exegetical Fallacies*, 59.

that θεός is λόγος. What is the implication that John applies a definite θεός to the λόγος? It communicates identity directly. It directly identifies who the λόγος is. A statement of essence indirectly identifies the identity the λόγος as θεός because only God has the divine essence. Furthermore, the perspective that God is "some kind of plural unity…permits us to let the second and third clauses of John 1:1 stand side by side."[76] In conclusion, it has been demonstrated that a definite θεός is possible and feasible.

What about a qualitative θεός? Wallace states that qualitative θεός provides some sort of a balance or a parallel to the qualitative σάρξ (sarx) in 1:14.[77] It is true that σάρξ is a qualitative noun. It is also true that a balance suggests some affinity. However, a definite θεός carries the same meaning; for the identity of the λόγος as θεός implies that his essence is divine. In other words, a definite θεός contains within itself also the qualitative attribute. The fact that σάρξ is a qualitative noun does not require θεός to be so as well. Carson provides an objection against qualitative usage: "There is a perfectly service-able word in Greek for 'divine' (namely θεῖος)."[78] When discussing the appropriate translation of 1:1c, Wallace states that "divine is acceptable only if it is a term that can be applied only to true deity."[79] The same has been echoed by White.[80] Although the discussion was about the translation of θεός, it shows that their understanding of θεός is absolute and full deity that is

---

[76] Carson, *Exegetical Fallacies*, 60.
[77] Wallace, *Greek Grammar beyond the Basics*, 269.
[78] Carson, *The Gospel According to John*, 117.
[79] Wallace, *Greek Grammar beyond the Basics*, 269.
[80] White, *The Forgotten Trinity: Recovering the Heart of Christian Belief*, 57.

attributed to God alone and that cannot be applied to other beings, such as angels.[81] Even with this view of θεός being a qualitative noun, identity is unavoidable. The reason for this is that θεός is a unique noun, located in a unique context of the Gospel of John, the New Testament, and Old Testament monotheism. As Carson points out, in this case, qualitative attributes quickly become a statement of identity.[82]

What about indefinite θεός? Indefinite θεός would imply polytheism.[83] Could John have wanted to *communicate* a different god? The problem with this view is that the context of the Gospel of John is clear monotheism, whether in the Old Testament or the New Testament.[84] In fact, John has affirmed his monotheism repeatedly in the Gospel, such as 5:44 and 17:3. Furthermore, indefinite θεός is incompatible with the Prologue of John in which the λόγος is said to be an eternal person with God.[85] Moreover, it is incompatible with the rest of the Gospel of John in which the deity of the Son is clearly pronounced.[86] Finally, Wallace cites a study that shows that at the least anarthrous pre-verbal predicate nominative nouns that are indefinite are very rare and thus they require clear contextual evidence to support such a claim.[87] Could John have wanted to communicate a lesser deity or a different idea by utilizing the Greek article as a differentiator between the one true God and

---

[81] Wallace, *Greek Grammar beyond the Basics*, 269.

[82] Carson, *Exegetical Fallacies*, 59.

[83] Wallace, *Greek Grammar beyond the Basics*, 266.

[84] White, *The Forgotten Trinity: Recovering the Heart of Christian Belief*, 55-56.

[85] White, *The Forgotten Trinity: Recovering the Heart of Christian Belief*, 56.

[86] Wallace, *Greek Grammar beyond the Basics*, 267.

[87] Wallace, *Greek Grammar beyond the Basics*, 267.

the lesser deity? The reason for this question is that several scholars, notably Dunn, have suggested that John used the Greek article, or lack thereof, to create a new semantic category out of θεός to indicate that the λόγος is not the true God.[88] More on this will be discussed in the chapters examining Philo's writings. To this, Carson responds with the following: John's own construction is "common Greek usage" and not a deliberate attempt to manipulate the grammar to achieve a goal.[89] Even within the Prologue of John, it has been shown that anarthrous θεός applied to the Father. John applies articular θεός to the Son in John 20:28.

The author has collected all instances of θεός in the Gospel of John. All genitive instances such as the glory of God or the son of God have been excluded. The following are metrics concerning the use of the Greek article. Sixty-seven percent of the instances are articular. Seventy percent of the instances that apply to the Father are articular. Thirty percent of the instances that apply to the Father are anarthrous. The 30% account for about 11 anarthrous instances that are clearly applied to the Father. Seventy-seven percent of the instances that are not clearly classified to either the Father or the Son are definite. Thirty-three percent of the instances that are applied to the Son are articular. This accounts for one instance. The lower number of instances for the Son makes the statistics less accurate for the Son. However, the point remains that, in general, the distribution of instances suggests that being articular or anarthrous has nothing to do with the type of deity or lesser deity but instead with John's idiomatic usage of such construction. When

---

[88] Dunn, *Christology in the Making*, 241.
[89] Carson, *The Gospel According to John*, 137.

mapping the definite article with the case of the verb, nominative instances have a higher rate of being articular compared to accusative instances. Eighty percent of the nominative instances are articular compared to 50% of the accusative instances. Although this is not a complete test, it does suggest that the grammatical case of θεός is the driving force for whether the article is used or not. The point is that the indefinite usage is out of the question.

Does the rest of the Gospel of John communicate the deity of Christ? There is the reference in John 20:28 that was mentioned earlier. But the term θεός is not the only way to communicate the thought of John 1:1c. In John 8:58, Jesus said, πρὶν Ἀβραὰμ γενέσθαι ἐγὼ εἰμι (prin Abraam genesthai egō eimi). In the context of this passage and repeatedly throughout chapter 8, Jesus uttered the expression ἐγὼ εἰμι in a manner in which he identifies himself as the ἐγὼ εἰμι. This is seen in 8:24, 8:28, and 8:58. It is also used in 13:19. Only four clear references in the New Testament are used in that sense. In the LXX, only three references match that sense, Deut 32:39, Isa 41:4, and Isa 43:10. There are other passages, such as Isa 48:12, that use the same expression but only in Hebrew. From the four Johannine instances, 8:58 is chosen for a reason that will be apparent later. For that passage, one cannot help but recall the passage in Exod 3:14, say this to the people of Israel: I AM has sent me to you. Most scholars prefer connecting John 8:58 with any of the LXX passages mentioned above, such as the passages in Isaiah.[90] That does not mean that there is no path to Exod 3:14. It is an indirect path passing first through Isaiah where יְהוָה (YHWH) uses אֲנִי־הוּא (ʾănī-hū, I am he) in the same absolute sense that Jesus did

---

[90] Bruce, *The Gospel & Epistles of John*, 205.

in John 8:58.[91] At the end, the goal is attained with Jesus identifying himself with יְהוָה (YHWH). Wayne Grudem cites Hos 1:7 as an example that suggests "two separate persons, both of whom can be called Lord."[92]

However, there is more to John 8:58. The prime reason why Isaiah's path is preferred over Exodus is that the LXX renders the Exodus verse: ὁ ὢν ἀπέσταλκέν με πρὸς ὑμᾶς (ho ōn apestalken me pros hymas). The main objection is that either John should have used ὁ ὢν, the present participle of εἰμί, or the LXX should have read ἐγὼ εἰμι ἀπέσταλκέν με πρὸς ὑμᾶς (egō eimi apestalken me pros hymas). In other words, John must have been restricted by the LXX rendering. When examining the original phrase in Hebrew, אֶהְיֶה ('ɛhyɛh, I exist/I am) is Qal imperfect, 1st person singular that is best translated as ἐγὼ εἰμι. Moreover, ἐγὼ εἰμι in John 8:58 is about existence. This makes אֶהְיֶה ('ɛhyɛh) the appropriate reference not אֲנִי־הוּא ('ǎnī-hū). This might suggest that John is not restricted by the LXX but somehow when the Hebrew serves his purpose, he is more willing to go that path. This is more evidence that John was not restricted by the LXX. When all the evidence is accumulated from many references, it is more than just a coincidence. The conclusion of 8:58 is that Jesus Christ has identified himself with יְהוָה (YHWH). This supports the conclusion of John 1:1c.

---

[91] White, *The Forgotten Trinity: Recovering the Heart of Christian Belief*, 98-99.

[92] Wayne Grudem, *Systematic Theology* (Grand Rapids: Zondervan, 1994), 228.

The Trinity

John 1:1, when placing all three clauses together, paints a picture about the λόγος. He is an eternal distinct person from the Father and yet he is united fully with him in essence. While the Father and the λόγος are the same God, they are distinct persons; who exist in eternal relationship. Carson states that John 1:1 contains "some of the crucial constituents of a full-blown doctrine of the Trinity."[93]

John 1:2 states: He was in the beginning with God. F. F. Bruce understands this verse not as a repetition of the first one, but as "the one who, according to the earlier scriptures, was with God in the beginning."[94] Bruce proceeds by connecting this passage with personified wisdom passages in the Old Testament, such as Proverbs 8.[95] Although this verse might not seem to support that claim now, it might be possible when taking in consideration the larger context of the Prologue and the Gospel of John. Moreover, if it is a reference to the OT, it is probably a reference to the entire Old Testament declaration of the Son and not just to a specific wisdom passage. As will be demonstrated, the constituents of the doctrine of the Trinity are clearly taught in the Old Testament.

---

[93] Carson, *The Gospel According to John*, 117.
[94] Bruce, *The Gospel & Epistles of John*, 31.
[95] Bruce, *The Gospel & Epistles of John*, 31.

Many passages in the Old Testament communicate the concept that God is not one person but that there are eternal persons in the one God. This is important because the exegesis of John 1:1 suggests that the Prologue of John taught a Trinitarian concept of God. An ideal background would support such a concept. One example that supports that concept is Isa 48:12-13,16:

> Listen to me, O Jacob, and Israel, whom I called! I am he; I
> am the first, and I am the last. My hand laid the foundation
> of the earth, and my right hand spread out the heavens; when
> I call to them, they stand forth together… Draw near to me,
> hear this: from the beginning I have not spoken in secret,
> from the time it came to be I have been there." And now the
> Lord GOD has sent me, and his Spirit.

The speaker is the Lord who clearly declares himself the first and the last. He also uses the absolute wording 'I am he.' In Isa 44:6, it explicitly states that the Lord יְהוָה (YHWH) affirms that he is the first and the last. There is no confusion that the speaker is יְהוָה (YHWH) in this passage (Isa 48:12). In Isa 48:13, he states that he is the creator. In Isa 44:24, it states, "I am the LORD, who made all things, who alone stretched out the heavens, who spread out the earth by myself." Therefore, there is no doubt that the Lord is the speaker, the Lord is the creator, and he alone is the creator. In verses 14 and 15, he continues to speak in context without interruption. In verse 16, the sender who is יְהוָה (YHWH) states that יְהוָה (YHWH) has sent him and his Spirit. It is possible that the Spirit is the sender or is sent with the speaker. Is there a possibility that a speaker has changed? This cannot be. Consider the following: If there were a change in speaker, a different speaker needs to be in verses 1-8; a change in verse 9 is needed until verse 13. Then a change is needed in verse 14. The change in speakers in verse 9 interrupts the speaker in his subject. However, it is not possible to go back to any verse earlier than verse 3, for the subject from verses 3-8 makes the speaker of verses 3-8 to be the speaker of verses 14-16. All of this makes it impossible that there was a change in speaker. Furthermore, to have the speaker changed just in verse 16 interrupts the flow of the whole chapter. Moreover, even if there was a change in speaker, what is spoken in verse 16 is typically spoken by the Lord in Isaiah. The first clause is similar to what the Lord has spoken in Isa 34:1. The second clause is parallel to what was spoken by the Lord in Isa 45:19. Even verse 15 is parallel to Isa 52:6. The emphasis that comes from double אֲנִי is only associated with the Lord in the Old Testament. John Oswalt states about verse 16a the following, "I see no way in which the subject of the first part of the verse could be the prophet. The things said there can be said only by God."[96] The consensus of the Early Church Fathers including Origen, Jerome, Theodoret of Cyr, Augustine, Cyril of Alexandria, and Ephrem the Syrian is this verse about the Trinity.[97] That does not always imply that their interpretation is correct. However, in this case, it is. On the other hand, two possibilities have been suggested by those who reject that interpretation. First, the possibility that there was a speaker change in the midst of verse 16! Second, the possibility that the text was corrupted somehow. The second possibility has absolutely no evidence whatsoever. It is a pure speculation despite all available Qumran manuscripts that has that text, namely 4Q58 and 1QIsaa, show continuity and

---

[96] John N. Oswalt. *The Book of Isaiah.* (Grand Rapids: Eerdmans 1998), 277-278.
[97] Mark Elliott, *Ancient Christian Commentary: Isaiah 40-66* (Intervarsity Press, 2007), 106.

no interruption or corruption. Nevertheless, it is relatively understandable why some scholars will appeal to the second possibility given the alternative: The first possibility is frankly too absurd. If there is a hint of feasibility in the first possibility, why anyone would appeal to the second one. There are many reasons for the difficulty of the first possibility. First, the change of speaker is very difficult in verse 16 for it is connected together with וְעַתָּה (wə'attāh). It is a logical conjunction that occurs about 270 times in the OT. In examining all of the instances, all of them without exception demonstrated strong dependency on the previous sentence or thought. All of them were part of a discourse where the speaker never changed. It never started a new topic or new speech but always was a continuation of what the speaker was preaching, praying, instructing, etc. Furthermore, it does not have an indication of starting a new speaker or a new subject. Second, a parallel within the verse brings it together. It is based on the words: עֵת ('ēṯ) and עַתָּה ('attāh). In particular, the speaker states that from that time, he was there and now he is sent. Third, 16b suggests that the person sent is of the same value as the spirit of the Lord. Grudem proposes that Isa 48:16 is a reference to the Trinity in the Old Testament.[98] John Mueller affirms the same.[99] It is a fact that the author of the Gospel of John was very familiar with the book of Isaiah, for he quoted and alluded to this book repeatedly. This is not evidence that John had this passage in mind when writing the Prologue of John, but it is evidence that the book of Isaiah, which is a quoted book in this Gospel, contains similar concepts and allusions.

---

[98] Grudem, *Systematic Theology*, 228.
[99] John Theodore Mueller, *Christian Dogmatics* (St. Louis: Concordia Publishing House, 1934), 159.

The Creator

John 1:3 states the following: All things were made through him, and without him was not anything made that was made. The λόγος was the creator of all things and therefore he was not created. Carson states, "Verse 3 simply insists, both positively and negatively, that the Word was God's agent in the creation of all that exists."[100] Bultmann claims that what is intended here by πάντα is ὁ κόσμος (panta is ho kosmos).[101] But this is not convincing because the sphere of creation in the context of God and eternity includes everything and not just the world as humans know it. Westcott states that the term ὁ κόσμος was avoided purposefully.[102] Brown says, "The expression "all" (panta) in verse 3 is quasi-liturgical formula which captures the fullness of God's creation."[103] It is very vital to explain what is meant and what is not meant by this. For the term "agent of creation" has meant different things in various religious and philosophical systems. There seems to be no better quotation to express the Johannine intention from verse 3 than what Schnackenburg has asserted about the λόγος:

---

[100] Carson, *The Gospel According to John*, 118.
[101] Bultmann, *The Gospel of John: A Commentary*, 37.
[102] Westcott, *The Gospel According to St. John*, 4.
[103] Brown, *The Gospel According to John: Introduction, Translation, and Notes*, 25.

He is not merely a way of speaking of the creative power of God or of the forms according to which God created the world. Since he is fully divine, he cannot be reduced to an intermediate stage; since he is a person, he cannot be dissolved into an idea.[104]

The New Testament state the same thing in Col 1:16-17:

> For by him all things were created, in heaven and on earth, visible and invisible, whether thrones or dominions or rulers or authorities - all things were created through him and for him. And he is before all things, and in him all things hold together.

The declaration that the Son was the creator of all things and that he was not created is strongly emphasized in that passage and in the Prologue.

The concept of the creator that is found in John reflects the Old Testament worldview. For in Gen 1:1, God created the heavens and the earth. In Isa 44:24, it was the Lord alone by himself who created and no one helped him. Pro 30:4 answers that question in the following way: What is his name, and what is the name of his Son. Evans suggests that this is what lies behind the expression, 'the son of man' in the Gospel of John.[105] This is so because John 3:13 alludes directly to it. This is consistent with the plurality found in Gen 1:26. Grudem proposes that the plurality cannot be explained as God talking to angels or as a form of majestic speech; but the best explanation

---

[104] Schnackenburg, *The Gospel According to St. John*, 241.

[105] Evans, *Word and Glory: On the Exegetical and Theological Background of John's Prologue*, 95.

is the existence of "a plurality of persons in God himself."[106] Muller[107] and Millard Erickson[108] state the same. If God and his Son are one in essence and united in the Godhead, then this is consistent with the rest of the Old Testament. This is the message of the Prologue of John: God the Father and God the Son are united even in creation.

---

[106] Grudem, *Systematic Theology*, 227.
[107] Mueller, *Christian Dogmatics*, 159.
[108] Millard J. Erickson, *Christian Theology* (Grand Rapids: Baker Books, 1998), 353-354.

Life (ζωή)

John 1:4 states that in the λόγος was life: In him was life. There are several observations to be said about this verse. First, the copulative verb ἦν was used. In the context of the prior three verses and in contrast to the verb ἐγένετο, it is reasonable to state that in λόγος was ζωή (zōē, life) eternally. The Gospel states, in many locations, that Jesus is the ζωή; as the following examples will show. It is noteworthy that Jesus being the life is not about his identity or his essence. But that he is the source of life. At the same time, it is more than just the fact that he contains life: as such there is a point in which he did not contain the life. But the Son is the eternal source of life. Second, that life was the source of light for others. Verse 1:4b suggests that the Son is the source of life for others and the life that he disperses to others was the source of light for them. Evidently, there is an element of dispersal in this text from the Son to the world.[109] There are many applications starting from this immediate context of creation in verse 3.[110] However, this verse encompasses more than just creation. The Son is the ultimate and eternal source of all physical and spiritual life. In this immediate context, it is about creation, but later in the Gospel, the spiritual life becomes the more dominant theme. The Gospel of John provides many parallels to this. In John 11:25-26, Jesus declares that he is ἡ

---

[109] Carson, *The Gospel According to John*, 119.
[110] Carson, *The Gospel According to John*, 119.

ζωή, whoever believes in him, even if he dies, shall live again, but those who are still living and believe, shall never die. Verse 25 states that Jesus is the ζωή and whoever believes in him, even if he dies, he will live. This is an indication that he will be resurrected by Jesus physically. This is a reference to the fact that Jesus is the source of life in terms of creation and physical resurrection. However, John 1:4b states that Jesus is the source of life for those who believe and thus they will never die. This is a reference to the fact that Jesus is the source of spiritual life. In John 6:35, Jesus declares that he is the bread of life; whoever comes and believes in him shall never be thirsty or hungry. The same idea is repeated in John 6:51 and many other verses. The conclusion is that Jesus is the source of life. He is the source of physical and spiritual life.

The best passage that articulates the concept of life is found in the early chapters of Genesis. Gen 2:9 states that the tree of life was in the midst of the garden. In Gen 2:17, God warned Adam and Eve not to eat from the tree of the knowledge of good and evil, because if they did, they would surely die on the day they ate. Afterwards, Adam and Eve ate from the tree of knowledge of good and evil. In Gen 3:22, God said that he would prevent them from eating from the tree of life, lest they ate and lived forever. The observation here is that when Adam and Eve ate from the wrong tree, they did not die physically right away. Instead, they died spiritually. In response to their spiritual death, God proceeded to prevent them from eating from the tree of life so that they would not live. It is possible that what God meant was that the tree of life would enable them to live physically forever since their physical life was cut short. However, the text emphasizes immediate instant death, and that the remedy was to eat from the tree of life. In other words, in order for them to live spiritually, they needed to eat of the tree of life. In the Prologue of John, the λόγος is described in John 1:4 as the source of life. The Gospel of John explains the meaning of this in the words of Jesus: He is the source of life and those who eat of him shall never die. This seems to echo the text of Genesis about the instant spiritual death of Adam and Eve; and how they needed to eat of the tree of life in order to live forever.

Light (φῶς)

In John 1:4-5, the text states: and the life was the light of men. The light shines in the darkness, and the darkness has not overcome it. It is important to realize that τὸ φῶς (to phōs, the light) refers back to verse 4b. In this verse, φῶς (phōs) refers to whatever it referred to in verse 4. It could refer to moral light, light of revelation, light of conscious or spiritual light. All of these applications come from the life whose source is the Son. The light shining in the darkness suggests that light in the world is not a quality of the world. But it is only given by God. Otherwise, there is darkness. This is similar to reading Gen 1:2-3 in that God is the creator of physical light and without the light, the state of creation is darkness. Isa 9:2 is an example of the light of the Messiah being shown to them. Concerning κατέλαβεν (katelaben), every instance of that verb in the New Testament has been researched, and the meanings of them are either 'overtake' (overcome) or 'comprehend'. Moreover, there is only one mention of that verb in the context of light in the New Testament and the LXX: John 12:35. In that verse, the light was there for a short period. As long as the light is with them, the darkness is not able to overtake them. But when the light is gone, then darkness overtakes them. This might suggest several things. First, the light cannot be overcome by the state of darkness. As long as the light is shining, it will continue to shine. Second, there is a hint of dualism, especially if the whole context of the Gospel of John is taken into consideration. But this is not a dualism in which two equal opposing forces exist side by side. Technically, dualism is not between darkness and light, for wherever the light chooses to shine, darkness cannot overcome it. It is more about humans' response to the light; and based on their attitude toward light, they are classified as the sons of light or sons of darkness.   Third, the relationship of light with darkness is equivalently sophisticated to the picture given in Genesis 1 and Isaiah 9. If the whole teaching of the Gospel of John concerning light and darkness is taken into consideration, it is not an entirely different system than the one taught in the Old Testament concerning sin, righteousness, and the attitude of humans toward the percepts of God.

In John 1:9, the text states: The true light, which gives light to everyone, was coming into the world. The λόγος is described as the τὸ φῶς τὸ ἀληθινόν (to phōs to alēthinon). Carson states that there is a contrast between how the Law and Wisdom give light and the λόγος, for the λόγος "is *the* light, the true light, the genuine and ultimate self-disclosure of God to man."[111] Carson explains, in that context, that the light is not just true and real in contrast with what is false, but with the previous provisions.[112] If the λόγος is the ultimate light who lights the world, this implies that he is the source of light. In Psa 36:9, God is described to be the fountain of life, in whose light people are able to see. The relationship between life and light has similarity to John 1:4. In Psa 43:3, God is asked to send his light for guidance. Ps 89:15 talks about the blessed people who walk in the light of the Lord. In Isa 2:5, the text states, "Let us walk in

---

[111] Carson, *The Gospel According to John*, 122.
[112] Carson, *The Gospel According to John*, 122.

the light of the Lord." The phrase ἐρχόμενον εἰς τὸν κόσμον (erchomenon eis ton kosmon) needs special attention. For ἐρχόμενον is a present middle participle and can be parsed as either accusative masculine singular or nominative neuter singular. Therefore, it can be describing either φῶς or ἄνθρωπον. Since the phrase comes directly after ἄνθρωπον, one might expect that that is what is being described. However, both Carson[113] and Bruce[114] prefer the former, for this expression commonly describes Jesus in the Gospel of John. In particular, John 3:19 and 12:46 describe Jesus as the light coming to the world. This phrase adds another flavor. It speaks of the incarnation of the Son. The text suggests an association between light and incarnation: the incarnation of the Son is a great light because the source of light has come to the world. In the context of messianic prophecies, in Isa 9:2 the people who walked in darkness saw a great light. In Isaiah 60, the Lord is the eternal light. In summary, in the Old Testament, the Lord himself is the ultimate light of the world. That light is promised to the world with the coming of the Messiah.

---

[113] Carson, *The Gospel According to John*, 121-122.
[114] Bruce, *The Gospel & Epistles of John*, 40.

World (κόσμος)

John 1:10 states: He was in the world, and the world was made through him, yet the world did not know him. The first observation is the existence of an obvious link to the preceding verse in which the λόγος is described as coming into the world. Therefore, ἐν τῷ κόσμῳ ἦν (en tō kosmō ēn) is to be understood from the context that the λόγος came to the world.[115] The second observation is that ἦν is utilized and it is contrasted to ἐγένετο; yet, it does not imply eternity. The reason for this is because he came into the world at a certain point in time and the world is not eternal. The third observation is that there is an epic drama of rejection. What John has described should be a major incident in the history of the world; and yet the majority of the world did not recognize him, in spite of the fact that he came to the world, was in the world and the world was created through him. From the perspective of John, it is the greatest irony of the history of the world. The fourth observation is that there is a sense of expectation on the part of John that the world should have recognized him. This is implied, of course.

John 1:11 continues with the same thought of rejection. It states, he came to his own and his own people did not receive him. This time the rejection came from his people, namely the Jewish people. The reason for the intentional specification is the

---

[115] Carson, *The Gospel According to John*, 124.

following: First, the Gospel of John was written to the Jewish people. This will be discussed in the Semitic chapters. Second, the numerous quotations, references and allusions to the Old Testament throughout the Gospel suggest that there was an expectation that the Jewish people would accept him because the Scriptures talk about him. Third, the Old Testament spoke numerous times of the special personal relationship between the Lord and his people. In the mind of John, his people should have recognized and accepted him. All of this adds up to the irony that even his people did not accept him. This seems to be almost an echo of Isaiah 53. In particular, Isa 53:8 states, "and as for his generation, who considered that he was cut off out of the land of the living, stricken for the transgression of my people?"

John 1:12 states: But to all who did receive him, who believed in his name, he gave the right to become children of God. After many verses beginning with καὶ (kai), the first δὲ (de) appears in the Prologue. In fact, it is the only one in the Prologue. In this context, this conjunction gives us a contrasting connectivity to verses 10 and 11. Yes, he was not recognized and was rejected, yet some accepted him. To those who receive him, namely those who believe in his name, he gave the right to τέκνα θεοῦ γενέσθαι (tekna theou genesthai). Carson suggests that John maintains a difference between τέκνα (tekna, children) and υἱός (huios, son).[116] The former is for those who receive him. The latter is for the unique Son of God. Verse 13 introduces the spiritual birth by which a person becomes a member of the family of God.

---

[116] Carson, *The Gospel According to John*, 126.

Flesh (σάρξ)

John 1:14 states that the λόγος became σάρξ (sarx, flesh). This declaration provides a particular worldview that is different from those systems that associate the physical world with evil and the spiritual world with good. The fact that the eternal Son who is fully God became σάρξ provides a sharp contrast to systems such as Gnosticism that require intermediate spiritual mediators to move from the spiritual to the physical realm. The verb, ἐσκήνωσεν (eskēnōsen, encamped), is used only in John 1:14 and four times in the book of Revelation. Searching the LXX, this verb is only found in Gen 13:12 which is irrelevant to the discussion. Expanding the search beyond the LXX, there is an equivalent Hebrew verb to ἐσκήνωσεν: שָׁכַן (šāḵan). שָׁכַן (šāḵan) is associated with the tabernacle or the tent of the meeting in its noun form, and even the Greek LXX rendering of that term is relevant. The idea is that as the Lord chose to dwell among his people; he chose to dwell closer by becoming flesh.[117] There are other examples that illustrate that point, such as Exod 25:8-9. Searching the Hebrew Old Testament for verses in which the Lord dwells among his people using the verb שָׁכַן (šāḵan), many relevant verses are found. For example, In Exod 25:8, the LXX renders the Hebrew verb as ὀφθήσομαι (ophthēsomai); other verses were rendered as κατασκηνόω

---

[117] Carson, *The Gospel According to John*, 127.

(kataskēnoō). From those verses, Zech 2:10-11(ESV) is a very relevant prophetic passage:

> Sing and rejoice, O daughter of Zion, for behold, I come and I will dwell in your midst, declares the LORD. And many nations shall join themselves to the LORD in that day, and shall be my people. And I will dwell in your midst, and you shall know that the LORD of hosts has sent me to you.

This passage is a prophecy about יְהֹוָה (YHWH) in which he will, in the future, come and dwell (וְשָׁכַנְתִּי, wəšāḵantī) in the midst of the daughter of Zion. Immediately in the next verse, יְהֹוָה reiterates the promise of dwelling and declares that יְהֹוָה (YHWH) has sent him, namely יְהֹוָה (YHWH). This is an example of the Father sending the Son. The speaker cannot be the prophet because he directly identifies himself as the Lord. A common theme in the Gospel of John is that the Son was sent by the Father. Based on the incarnation alone, most of the candidate backgrounds would not meet the criteria. Bruce describes John's declaration of the incarnation in the following words, "no declaration would have been so uncompromisingly anti-docetic." [118] Another description is "real historical human person."[119] Why is this important? It is so for two reasons. First, the candidate backgrounds whose worldview is built on the separation of the physical from the spiritual do not provide the logical background for John. Second, a primary candidate background needs to have the anticipation of visitation by God himself in the form of a "real historical human person."[120]

---

[118] Bruce, *The Gospel & Epistles of John*, 40.
[119] Bruce, *The Gospel & Epistles of John*, 40.
[120] Bruce, *The Gospel & Epistles of John*, 40.

Several passages, prophecies, and illustrations can be drawn from the Old Testament to demonstrate that the Lord will become flesh. For example, the birth of Emmanuel is prophesized in Isa 7:14. Within the same context, Isa 9:6 demonstrates that the Messiah is God and that God will be incarnated, "For to us a child is born, to us a son is given, and the government will be on his shoulders. And he will be called Wonderful Counselor, Mighty God, Everlasting Father, Prince of Peace." The simple reading of this passage declares that the Messiah is God. There are several observations about the Hebrew word אֵל (ʾēl). The context suggests that the best translation of אֵל (ʾēl) is God. Especially, when taking into consideration: גִּבּוֹר אֲבִיעַד (gibbōr ʾăḇīʿaḏ). While גִּבּוֹר (gibbōr) has been used to describe humans, it has certainly been applied to God in Psa 24:8, Psa 45:3, Isa 10:21, and Zeph 3:17. Furthermore, when it is combined with אֵל (ʾēl), it is only used of God. The only other instance is in Isa 10:21, a reference to the Lord. אֲבִיעַד (ʾăḇīʿaḏ) is a unique expression in the Hebrew text. It is best translated as 'the father of everlastingness.' Another example is Psalm 45 in which the Messiah is called God.

Unique & Beloved (μονογενής)

In John 1:14 the λόγος is described as μονογενοῦς from the Father. Unfortunately, μονογενοῦς (μονογενής, monogenēs, unique and beloved) has been translated in the past as 'only begotten' which did not help the exegesis of the passage but added more confusion to it.[121] BDAG suggests the meaning of 'unique.'[122] The puzzle that needs to be answered is can a clear instance of a background passage, in which μονογενής is intersected with the subject of a relationship between a father and a son, be found. None is found in the LXX. When the search is widened to include the New Testament, only one passage is found: Heb 11:17, about Abraham offering his μονογενής son. This would be an ideal passage, equivalent to Gen 22:2. The LXX uses ἀγαπητός (agapētos, beloved) instead of μονογενής to translate the Hebrew word יָחִיד. This is evidence that the book of Hebrews did not utilize the LXX for that particular passage, but probably used the Hebrew Old Testament instead. Could it be possible that the author of the Gospel of John was not restricted by the LXX? If this is not the case, why would two New Testament authors prefer to use a different Greek word than the one utilized by the LXX? Hebrews' passage associated with Gen 22:2 strongly suggests that Gen 22:2 is the true background of the Johannine's use of μονογενής. This is confirmed later with

---

[121] D.A. Carson, *Exegetical Fallacies*, 30-32.
[122] BDAG, s.v. "μονογενοῦς."

the tight association of μονογενής with יָחִיד (yāḥīḏ). Therefore, to understand the meaning of μονογενής, one has to understand the Hebrew equivalent, יָחִיד (yāḥīḏ). [123] Moreover, it is associated primarily with the usage of יָחִיד (yāḥīḏ) in Gen 22:2. If one would claim that Gen 22:2 is an exception to the true meaning of μονογενής, then this exception is the only relevant passage for the background of μονογενής in John. Nevertheless, as will be demonstrated later, it is not an exception.

In order to answer these questions, a search needs to be performed to find the full semantic range and usage of μονογενής and יָחִיד (yāḥīḏ). All verses in the LXX that contain μονογενής have יָחִיד (yāḥīḏ) in the corresponding Hebrew verses. All Hebrew verses that have יָחִיד (yāḥīḏ) are translated by the LXX as either μονογενής or ἀγαπητός with the exception of one irrelevant instance of μονοτρόπους. There are several significant observations:

1. None of the the references of μονογενής in the LXX is tied to the idea of begotten, generation, or birth of the Hebrew OT. They are all tied to the Hebrew יָחִיד (yāḥīḏ). Its meaning will be discussed later.

2. There are many Hebrew words that express the idea of begotten: יָלוּד (yəlūḏ) (LXX translated as: τεχθείς, παιδίον, γεννητὸς), יְלִיד (yəlīḏ) (LXX translated as: οἰκογενεῖς), נוֹלַד (nōlaḏ) (LXX: τοῦ γενομένου, τίκτεται), יוּלָּד (yūllāḏ) (LXX: τῷ

---

[123] Carson, *The Gospel According to John*, 128.

τικτομένῳ). Yet none of them is translated μονογενής.

3. For the other direction, none of Hebrew יָחִיד (yāḥīḏ) is translated γεννηθεὶς or any equivalent in LXX. It is either μονογενής or ἀγαπητός (and one instance of μονοτρόπους). This suggests that these two words are possibly interchangeable for the semantic meaning of יָחִיד (yāḥīḏ).

4. If the search of the LXX is expanded to include second temple literature, all of the references match the context of the OT passages of the way יָחִיד (yāḥīḏ) was utilized. In other words, if there would be Hebrew translation, יָחִיד (yāḥīḏ) would be the Hebrew word that best and consistently explain the meaning.

Therefore, there is some affinity between μονογενής and ἀγαπητός. The LXX renders Gen 22:2, your only son Isaac, whom you love, as τὸν υἱόν σου τὸν ἀγαπητόν ὃν ἠγάπησας. There is a redundant repetition that it not intended by the Hebrew text. It is true that יָחִיד (yāḥīḏ) has the idea of 'beloved', which is why the LXX utilizes ἀγαπητός. But יָחִיד (yāḥīḏ) communicates the idea of uniqueness as well, and since the text already communicates the idea of Abraham loving his Son, μονογενής is a more appropriate translation than ἀγαπητός. No wonder the author of the book of Hebrews chose not to follow the LXX. It is reasonable that the author of the Gospel of John is not restricted by the LXX either. Based on this working assumption, if the Hebrew Old Testament is searched for all the verses that contain the word יָחִיד (yāḥīḏ) and contain the subject of the relationship between a father and a son, only three verses are found; all of them are in Gen 22: the passage about Abraham and Isaac. John was using the experience of Abraham and Isaac to communicate a picture of the personal relationship between the Father and the λόγος. This picture is amplified in later passages, such as John 3:16.

Careful examination of each instance of יָחִיד (yāḥīḏ) suggest the semantic domain of it. Let the consensus of the great dictionary articulate the point. HALOT gives us the following range for יָחִיד (yāḥīḏ): only, beloved, lonely, unique. This semantic range is confirmed by checking the Dictionary of Classical Hebrew, Kohlenberger/Mounce and BDB. It is remarkable that the Arabic equivalent to יָחִיד (yāḥīḏ) is وحيد (Wahid). The literal meaning of وحيد is only one. It carries within it the idea that it is a person who is unique, precious and greatly beloved. There is no element of birth or generation in it.

Concerning the New Testament, there is a clear reference to Christ as "born." It is in Gal 4:4, born of woman. But here γενόμενον is used. In fact, the New Testament is rich of Greek words to express every subtlety born (γενόμενον), firstborn (πρωτότοκος), heir (κληρονόμον), and others. There are already serviceable words for them.

This should be sufficient to establish the meaning of μονογενής in the New Testament. Yet recently, some have challenged such exegesis:

First, An appeal to Justin Martyr:

Μονογενὴς γὰρ ὅτι ἦν τῷ Πατρὶ τῶν ὅλων οὗτος, ἰδίως ἐξ αὐτοῦ Λόγος καὶ δύναμις γεγενημένος, καὶ ὕστερον ἄνθρωπος διὰ τῆς Παρθένου γενόμενος, ὡς ἀπὸ τῶν ἀπομνημονευμάτων ἐμάθομεν, προεδήλωσα.[124]

Charles Lee Irons claims Μονογενής has to be translated begotten because the text states that the Son is μονογενής of the Father by being begotten.125 There are several problems with this assertion:

1. It is not sufficient to establish one or several instances of μονογενής meaning only begotten. Instead must establish one of the two:

2. All occurrences of μονογενής mean only begotten. He concedes this point.[126]

3. Some of the occurrences of μονογενής mean 'only begotten' and the instances in the New Testament can only mean 'only begotten'. This will be examined.

4. It is not sufficient to establish that an instance of μονογενής can possibly mean "only begotten." There must be sufficient evidence that it cannot mean unique or beloved. There is a logical fallacy with the assertion in question. The simplistic statement that 'the Son is the μονογενής of the Father because he was begotten' does not imply

---

[124] Justin Martyr, *Dialog With Trypho*, 105.
[125] Charles Lee Irons, "A Lexical Defense Of The Johannine Only Begotten," in *Retrieving Eternal Generation*, ed. Fred Sanders and Scott R. Swain, (Zondervan 2017) 102.
[126] Irons, "A Lexical Defense Of The Johannine Only Begotten," in *Retrieving Eternal Generation*, 105.

that μονογενής here means begotten. It is possible to interpret that statement that the Son is unique one of the Father because he was begotten." This statement does not count as a legitimate evidence for 'only begotten.'

5. The context suggests that it cannot mean "only begotten" but "unique." What Justin actually say: The Son is the μονογενής of the Father because he was begotten and having later become a man through the virgin. In other words, there are two reasons why he is μονογενής of the Father: being born and also the incarnation through a virgin. It is unthinkable that the Son is begotten of the Father because he was incarnated through a virgin. Justin is speaking about the uniqueness of the Son. He is the unique one of the Father through his special unique relationship to the Father and through his unique incarnation from a virgin. This may suggest that this evidence counts towards "unique" and not towards "only begotten."

Second: Appeal to Latin127, Etymology128, and Lexical arguments129:

---

[127] Irons, "A Lexical Defense Of The Johannine Only Begotten," in *Retrieving Eternal Generation*, 100, 112.

[128] Irons, "A Lexical Defense Of The Johannine Only Begotten," in *Retrieving Eternal Generation*, 103-105.

[129] Irons, "A Lexical Defense Of The Johannine Only Begotten," in *Retrieving Eternal Generation*, 105-111.

Appealing to Latin suggests that there is not enough evidence in Greek. I will let Carson responds to the etymology argument:

> Nowadays we all know that etymology is a horribly unreliable way to determine the meaning of words, best reserved for rare words that show up so infrequently we have too few contexts to help determine their meaning.[130]

I will respond to the Lexical argument. After failing to establish one single Hellenistic reference that clearly demonstrates that μουνογενής is 'only begotten', he suggests:

> My claim is that μονογενής is used most basically and frequently in reference to an only child begotten by a parent, with the implications of not having any siblings. A base/profile analysis puts the term in a biological familial context. It presupposes a biological relationship between a parent and his or her only son or daughter.[131]

He further adds:

> If the word meant "only," then we would expect to find it used to modify many other nouns that do not involve the context of being begotten or being an offspring, for example, "only wife," "only brother," "only friend…"[132]

The following are the responses:

---

[130] D.A. Carson, "John 5:26: Cruz Interpretum for Eternal Generation," in *Retrieving Eternal Generation*, ed. Fred Sanders, Scott R. Swain, (Zondervan, 2017) 88-89.

[131] Irons, "A Lexical Defense Of The Johannine Only Begotten," in *Retrieving Eternal Generation*, 106.

[132] Irons, "A Lexical Defense Of The Johannine Only Begotten," in *Retrieving Eternal Generation*, 106.

1. To argue against the μονογενής meaning 'only' is a strawman argument. The meaning is deeper: unique and beloved.

2. Arguing that μονογενής is most basically and frequently about only child is not sufficient. It is not replacement to finding actual occurrences of μονογενής that clearly mean 'only begotten" and further to show that the Biblical references are likewise.

3. This assertion ignores the evidence. For example, Tobit 8:17 mentions more than one child being μονογενής. LXX Psa 21:20 and 34:17 both suggest that they are possibly about a beloved wife rather than a daughter. Many examples can be provided that do not fit Iron's definition.

4. The assertion fails to understand the uniqueness and love aspect that makes it most appropriate for child/parent relationship. This is precisely because it ignores the usage of יָחִיד (yāḥīḏ) in the Hebrew text that was translated to the LXX. There is special focused love between a parent and a child, when that child is the only child or that child is unique one out of many. Furthermore, it suggests that the love is focused in one direction from the parent to the child. This becomes significant in the theology of the Gospel of John. This would explain why there are most instances of parent/child relationship when familial relationships are considered. This does not imply that μονογενής is confined in familial relationships.

Third: the claim that Isaac is the only child or the only heir:

Irons suggest the following:

In this case, an "only-begotten" son may actually have siblings and yet be his only father's legitimate son or heir and so it is as if he were an "only begotten" son.[133]

He further explains, "Sarah compels Abraham to disown Ishmael so that he is no longer an heir in competition with Isaac."[134] The following are the responses:

1. Irons has abandoned the criteria of begotten and switched to Heir. He applies this to 4 references in the LXX. This is problematic when the total number of occurrences in the LXX is 10 (19 with the NT). In other words, Irons justified 40% of occurrences that deviated from his system by appealing to an heir-based semantic. This is a major problem. The heir argument is consistent with uniqueness.

2. What complicates his explanation is that the heir is also the elder son even with multiple siblings. Then this fundamentally contradicts his definition that it is only begotten child when every family has a unique heir despite of the usual multiple siblings. This suggests according to Irons' definition, for those families with multiple siblings, heir is the

---

[133] Irons, "A Lexical Defense Of The Johannine Only Begotten," in *Retrieving Eternal Generation*, 108.
[134] Irons, "A Lexical Defense Of The Johannine Only Begotten," in *Retrieving Eternal Generation*, 108.

only criteria, while for those families with one child, 'only begotten' is the only criteria.

3. Furthermore, Carson states, "Abraham sired not only Ishmael and Isaac but several others by Keturah."[135] Therefore, this does not fit in Irons' framework.

4. Heb 11:17 does not describe the relationship between Sarah and Isaac but between Abraham and Isaac.

5. This is the most important references that requires establishing a clear and exclusive 'only begotten' meaning, for it forms the background of the Johannine references above.

Fourth: the claim that John 1:14,18 supports the rendering of 'only Begotten:'

Irons observes that in both references, some translations add 'Son' which is derived from the context. So he wonders "But why not go the whole way?"[136] Then he explains his loaded question that "from the Father" implies begotten from the Father.[137] In John 1:18, he attacked the rendering of the ESV.[138]

---

[135] Carson, "John 5:26: Cruz Interpretum for Eternal Generation," in *Retrieving Eternal Generation*, 90.

[136] Irons, "A Lexical Defense Of The Johannine Only Begotten," in *Retrieving Eternal Generation*, 113.

[137] Irons, "A Lexical Defense Of The Johannine Only Begotten," in *Retrieving Eternal Generation*, 113.

[138] Irons, "A Lexical Defense Of The Johannine Only Begotten," in *Retrieving Eternal Generation*, 114.

1. Irons ignores the background of John 1:14 in that it is a reference to Gen 22:2, in that the relationship between Abraham and Isaac is a type of that eternal relationship between the Father and the Son. Therefore, one should refer back to the Hebrew terms that are utilized, and the nature of the relationship: uniqueness and love.

2. The context and the background suggest the Sonship relationship. The Son is the unique and beloved of the Father precisely because he is the eternal beloved Son of the Father. Yet there is a difference between the term on one hand and the context and background on the other. Just because the Prologue of John is about the Son, and therefore, it seems appropriate to add the Son in these verses, that does not imply that μονογενής means son. In fact, a literal translation does not require the term son to be added. Extrapolating From Carson's commentary[139], "As the unique and beloved one from the Father" is to me the perfect rendition of it.

3. The fact that the Son is the son of the Father with an eternal relationship of uniqueness and love does not imply that he was begotten. While the expression, which is based on the background and the context, implies sonship, it does not imply that the Son is begotten, as much as יָחִיד (yāḥīḏ) in Gen 22:2 describing the relationship between Abraham Isaac is not begotten.

---

[139] Carson, *The Gospel According to John*, 134.

---

4. Concerning παρὰ πατρός, I looked at all verses in the Gospel of John that have παρὰ in them. 7:29 might be the closest one that expresses a theme based "παρὰ πατρός," ἐγὼ οἶδα αὐτόν, ὅτι παρ᾽ αὐτοῦ εἰμι κἀκεῖνός με ἀπέστειλεν. This has nothing to do with being begotten but with being sent from the Father.[140]

5. We do not have to guess the meaning of the expression, "μονογενοῦς παρὰ πατρός", there is a parallel text for it: "μονογενὴς θεὸς ὁ ὢν εἰς τὸν κόλπον τοῦ πατρὸς". Carson provides the best explanation:

The words translated who is at the Father's side in the NIV might more literally be rendered 'who is in the bosom of the Father'. A similar expression is found elsewhere: Lazarus is in Abraham's bosom (Lk. 16:22-23), and John rests on Jesus' bosom at the last supper (13:23). It apparently conveys an aura of intimacy, mutual love and knowledge.[141]

6. For the sake of argument, if there are any supposed rendering issues in a translation, that does not justify correcting it with even worse rendering, 'only begotten.' The best rendering I have seen is, "The unique and beloved one, [himself] God."[142]

Despite examining the LXX, the background for μονογενής, and the challenges to it, for the sake of completeness, various references about μονογενής were examined. I checked second temple pseudepigrapha and found several references. All the

---

[140] Carson, *The Gospel According to John*, 318.
[141] Carson, *The Gospel According to John*, 134.
[142] Carson, *The Gospel According to John*, 134.

references agree with the semantic domain suggested above. Here is an example, Aristobolus 4:3, εἰ μὴ μουνογενής τις ἀπορρὼξ φύλου ἄνωθεν Χαλδαίων. This directly means unique. I do not see how it can mean begotten.

When examining the references in Josephus, the four references are similar to Gen 22:2. They express the following meanings: unique, only, and beloved. I could not find any reference in Philo, but I found the term begotten; it utilizes terms such as γέννημα for it.

Then the apostolic fathers were examined. Three references were found. Two of the references utilize μονογενής as title for Christ. In general, for all church fathers utilization of μονογενής as a title, it is either a quotation of NT text, or mere title without explanation. In either case, they show dependency on the NT. They also are unhelpful in determining whether the intended meaning is begotten or otherwise. The third one is 1Clement 25:2:

> ὄρνεον γάρ ἐστιν, ὃ προσονομάζεται φοῖνιξ· τοῦτο μονογενὲς ὑπάρχον ζῇ ἔτη πεντακόσια· γενόμενόν τε ἤδη πρὸς ἀπόλυσιν τοῦ ἀποθανεῖν αὐτό, σηκὸν ἑαυτῷ ποιεῖ ἐκ λιβάνου καὶ σμύρνης καὶ τῶν λοιπῶν ἀρωμάτων, εἰς ὃν πληρωθέντος τοῦ ⌜χρόνου εἰσέρχεται καὶ τελευτᾷ

The above reference is important because out of 3 references, it is the only reference that gives positive meaning: unique kind. While this is only one reference, it is the only reference from the apostolic fathers.

Concerning Justin and Irenaeus, no reference that supports begotten. But in the first letter of Irenaeus 1:1, he describes an Aeon called Βυθὸς. He is described as, ὑπάρχοντα δ᾽ αὐτὸν ἀχώρητον καὶ ἀόρατον, ἀΐδιόν τε καὶ ἀγέννητον. Then Irenaeus proceeded to identity the titles that are given to him μονογενής along with 3 other entities which he called: Πυθαγορικὴν Τετρακτὺν. So Βυθὸς was both ἀγέννητον and μονογενής. This is direct evidence that μονογενής does not mean begotten. Previously, I argued against the meaning of begotten by listing every possibly reference in specific literature and showing that none of them can be utilized as an evidence for begotten. Now, there is a reference that suggests that it cannot be begotten.

Next, I scanned pre-Nicene church fathers, from Clement of Alexandria, to Hippolytus, to Origen. I found no support for begotten. Next, I examined apocryphal gospels, apocalypses and acts. No support for begotten. Then Pseudo-Clementine homilies; but no support for begotten. I Could not find anything relevant in Eusebius, Basil, and Gregory of Nyssa. This is despite the language of begotten in Gregory of Nyssa. Epiphanius states in support of unique:

Οὐ γὰρ πάρεστι τούτῳ οὐ πατὴρ ἐπὶ γῆς, οὐ φίλος, οὐ μαθητὴς, οὐ συγγενὴς, οὐκ ἐνταφιαστής· ἀλλ' αὐτὸς μόνος τοῦ μόνου μονογενής, ἐν κόσμῳ Θεὸς, καὶ ἄλλος οὐδείς.[143]

Concerning Athanasius and Gregory of Nazianzus, there are many passages that support unique: In Arians 2:19, ὡς μηκέτι κατ' αὐτοὺς Μονογενῆ εἶναι, ἀλλ' ἐκ πολλῶν ἀδελφῶν ἕνα. Also in Arians 2:48:

[143] J.-P. Migne, *Patrologiae cursus completus* (series Graeca) (MPG) 43, Paris: Migne, 1857-1866: 440-464. Retrieved from: http://stephanus.tlg.uci.edu/Iris/Cite?2021:013:13408

Πάλιν τε εἰ μονογενής ἐστι, πῶς ἀρχὴ τῶν ὁδῶν αὐτὸς γίνεται; Ἀνάγκη γάρ, αὐτὸν ἀρχὴν τῶν πάντων κτισθέντα, μηκέτι μόνον εἶναι, ἔχοντα τοὺς μετ᾽ αὐτὸν γενομένους. Καὶ γὰρ καὶ Ῥουβήμ, ἀρχὴ τῶν τέκνων γενόμενος, οὐκ ἦν μονογενής, ἀλλὰ τῷ μὲν χρόνῳ πρῶτος, τῇ δὲ φύσει καὶ τῇ συγγενείᾳ εἷς ὢν τῶν μετ᾽ αὐτὸν ἐτύγχανεν.

There is one passage that requires deeper dive; consider Arians 2:62:

Εἰ μὲν οὖν Μονογενής ἐστιν, ὥσπερ οὖν καὶ ἔστιν, ἑρμηνευέσθω τό, "πρωτότοκος·" εἰ δὲ πρωτότοκός ἐστι, μὴ ἔστω Μονογενής. Οὐ δύναται γὰρ ὁ αὐτὸς Μονογενής τε καὶ πρωτότοκος εἶναι, εἰ μὴ ἄρα πρὸς ἄλλο καὶ ἄλλο· ἵνα Μονογενὴς μὲν διὰ τὴν ἐκ Πατρὸς γέννησιν, ὥσπερ εἴρηται, πρωτότοκος δὲ διὰ τὴν εἰς τὴν κτίσιν συγκατάβασιν, καὶ τὴν τῶν πολλῶν ἀδελφοποίησιν. Ἀμέλει, τῶν δύο τούτων ῥητῶν ἀντικειμένων ἀλλήλοις, κρατεῖν ἄν τις εἴποι δικαίως ἐπὶ τοῦ Λόγου τὸ τοῦ Μονογενοῦς μᾶλλον ἰδίωμα, διὰ τὸ μὴ εἶναι ἕτερον Λόγον, ἢ ἄλλην σοφίαν, ἀλλὰ τοῦτον μόνον ἀληθινὸν Υἱὸν εἶναι τοῦ Πατρός

Athanasius' argument is the following: How can the Son be πρωτότοκος (one of many) when he is μονογενής (only one, or unique). He is arguing against Arians' assertion that he was the first one created out of many. His response is that he is unique in certain way and one of many in others. He adds that he is unique because he is generated by the Father. One thing clear, Athanasius seems to miss the OT background of πρωτότοκος. πρωτότοκος is בְּכֹר. It carries the idea of the heir so that the Son is not necessarily first born but the heir. Nevertheless, the question remains did Athanasius also contrast first-begotten versus only-begotten in his argument? Or was it only one-of-many versus unique? If the former is possible, then it is possible that Athanasius and others of the 4th century fathers have overloaded the term μονογενής theologically: He is unique because he was generated. Then consequently, μονογενής carries the semantic of begotten from added theological function in the 4th century A.D. However, Athanasius immediately adds this explanation:

> κρατεῖν ἄν τις εἴποι δικαίως ἐπὶ τοῦ Λόγου τὸ τοῦ Μονογενοῦς μᾶλλον ἰδίωμα, διὰ τὸ μὴ εἶναι ἕτερον Λόγον, ἢ ἄλλην σοφίαν, ἀλλὰ τοῦτον μόνον ἀληθινὸν Υἱὸν εἶναι τοῦ Πατρός.

He is μονογενής because the term means unique, as he put it later, "ὥστε τοῦ μὲν Πατρὸς εἶναι Μονογενῆ τὸν Υἱόν, διὰ τὸ ἐξ αὐτοῦ μόνον αὐτὸν εἶναι."[144] Therefore, this passage cannot be used in support of begotten.

The support for the meaning of unique increases with more citations from Athanasius, "Λόγος μὲν οὖν ὤν, ᾗ Λόγος ἐστίν, οὐκ ἔχει τοιούτους, οἷός ἐστι καὶ αὐτός, τοὺς συναρμολογουμένους αὐτῷ· μονογενὴς γάρ ἐστιν." [145] Furthermore, Athanasius brings the idea of beloved:

---

[144] Athanasius, *Arians*, 2:64.
[145] Athanasius, *Arians* 2:74.

Ταὐτὸν γάρ ἐστι τό τε Μονογενὲς καὶ τὸ Ἀγαπητόν, ὡς τό, "Οὗτός ἐστιν ὁ Υἱός μου ὁ ἀγαπητός." Οὐ γὰρ δὴ τὴν εἰς αὐτὸν ἀγάπην σημᾶναι θέλων, εἶπε τό, Ἀγαπητός, ἵνα μὴ τοὺς ἄλλους μισεῖν δόξῃ· ἀλλὰ τὸ Μονογενὲς ἐδήλου, ἵνα τὸ μόνον ἐξ αὐτοῦ εἶναι αὐτὸν δείξῃ. Καὶ τῷ Ἀβραὰμ γοῦν σημᾶναι θέλων ὁ Λόγος τὸ μονογενές, φησί· "Προσένεγκε τὸν υἱόν σου τὸν ἀγαπητόν." Παντὶ δὲ δῆλον, ἐκ τῆς Σάρρας μόνον εἶναι τὸν Ἰσαάκ Ταὐτὸν γάρ ἐστι τό τε Μονογενὲς καὶ τὸ Ἀγαπητόν, ὡς τό, "Οὗτός ἐστιν ὁ Υἱός μου ὁ ἀγαπητός." Οὐ γὰρ δὴ τὴν εἰς αὐτὸν ἀγάπην σημᾶναι θέλων, εἶπε τό, Ἀγαπητός, ἵνα μὴ τοὺς ἄλλους μισεῖν δόξῃ· ἀλλὰ τὸ Μονογενὲς ἐδήλου, ἵνα τὸ μόνον ἐξ αὐτοῦ εἶναι αὐτὸν δείξῃ. Καὶ τῷ Ἀβραὰμ γοῦν σημᾶναι θέλων ὁ Λόγος τὸ μονογενές, φησί· "Προσένεγκε τὸν υἱόν σου τὸν ἀγαπητόν." Παντὶ δὲ δῆλον, ἐκ τῆς Σάρρας μόνον εἶναι τὸν Ἰσαάκ.[146]

He does not equate it completely: Yes it means beloved but also Isaac was the only son of Sarah. However, this becomes more emphatic:

Τὸ δὲ ἀγαπητὸν καὶ Ἕλληνες ἴσασιν οἱ δεινοὶ περὶ τὰς λέξεις, ὅτι ἴσον ἐστὶ τῷ εἰπεῖν Μονογενής. Φησὶ γὰρ Ὅμηρος ἐπὶ Τηλεμάχου, τοῦ Υἱοῦ Ὀδυσσέως μονογενοῦς ὄντος, ταῦτα ἐν τῇ δευτέρᾳ τῆς Ὀδυσσείας. "Τίπτε δέ τοι, φίλε τέκνον, ἐνὶ φρεσὶ τοῦτο νόημα Ἔπλετο; πῇ δὲ θέλεις ἰέναι πολλὴν ἐπὶ γαῖαν, Μοῦνος ἐὼν ἀγαπητός; Ὁ δ᾽ ὤλετο τηλόθι πάτρης Διογενὴς Ὀδυσεύς, ἀλλογνώτων ἐνὶ δήμῳ." Ὁ ἄρα μόνος ὢν τῷ πατρὶ ἀγαπητὸς λέγεται.[147]

He appeals to secular Greeks to show that μονογενής and ἀγαπητός are ἴσον; closely related if not synonymous. In conclusion, μονογενής for Athanasius means both unique in nature and his relationship to the Father, and beloved. Likewise,

---

[146] Athanasius, *Arians* 4:24.
[147] Athanasius, *Arians* 4:29.

Gregory of Nazianzus states, "Μονογενὴς δέ, οὐχ ὅτι μόνος ἐκ μόνου καὶ μόνον, ἀλλ᾽ ὅτι καὶ μονοτρόπως, οὐχ ὡς τὰ σώματα."[148]

---

[148] Gregory of Nazianzus, *Oration* 30:20.

Full of Grace and Truth

John 1:14 states that the unique beloved Son is full of grace and truth. Evans suggests that Exodus 33-34 "clearly lies behind the second half of the Prologue (Jn 1.14-18)."[149] The best exegesis for this passage is presented by Carson.[150] The question is where is the manifestation of glory associated with πλήρης χάριτος καὶ ἀληθείας (plērēs charitos kai alētheias, full of grace and truth)? In Exodus 33-34, Moses asked the Lord יְהוָה (YHWH) to show him his glory. In the manifestation of glory of יְהוָה (YHWH), he was described as רַב־חֶסֶד וֶאֱמֶת (raḇ-ḥeseḏ wɛ'ĕmɛt). This phrase is typically translated as abounding in steadfast love and faithfulness or truth. חֶסֶד (ḥeseḏ) can be translated as steadfast love, favor, or grace. It is the closest Hebrew word for grace. אֱמֶת ('ĕmɛt) is translated as faithfulness or truth. In short, the latter part of John 1:14 provides a definite allusion to the incident in Exodus 33-34.

There are several conclusions that can be made from this. First, the λόγος is יְהוָה (YHWH). The expression רַב־חֶסֶד וֶאֱמֶת (raḇ-ḥeseḏ wɛ'ĕmɛt) has been used of God alone. In Exodus 33-34, it has been used in conjunction with the glory of the Lord. But Exodus is not the only passage that contains this phrase. It

---

[149] Evans, *Word and Glory: On the Exegetical and Theological Background of John's Prologue*, 79.
[150] Carson, *The Gospel According to John*, 129-130.

is used in Psa 86:15 to describe יְהוָה (YHWH). Therefore, the application of the expression, רַב־חֶסֶד וֶאֱמֶת (rab̲-ḥɛsɛd̲ wɛ'ɛmɛt̲), to the λόγος, and the association of the glory of Christ with the glory of יְהוָה (YHWH), provide us with more evidence to the identity of the λόγος. Second, the LXX translation for the expression in question is πολυέλεος καὶ ἀληθινὸς not πλήρης χάριτος καὶ ἀληθείας (polyeleos kai alēthinos not plērēs charitos kai alētheias). Yet John's translation is more literal for it keeps the nouns as nouns; and is better because it translatesחֶסֶד (ḥɛsɛd̲) as 'grace' instead of 'mercy.' The real question is why did not John utilize the LXX expression? The simple and most direct answer is that John was not restricted by the LXX, but that somehow he had access to the Hebrew Old Testament.[151]

Third, in Exod 33:20, the Lord said to Moses that he could not see his face because no one sees him and lives. This passage does not give any indication that Moses was talking to a smaller version of deity. In that passage, the deity and the glory of the Lord were not diminished in anyway. It was not an impersonal and limited manifestation of God, but the manifestation of the Lord himself. Fourth, in that passage, the entity that appeared to Moses was a person and not an impersonal force.

John 1:16-17 states that we have received from his fullness χάριν ἀντὶ χάριτος (charin anti charitos, grace instead of grace). What does the preposition ἀντὶ mean? This preposition occurs only once in the Gospel of John. It occurs about 20 times in the New Testament. In all of the occurrences in the New Testament, not one single instance means 'upon' or 'in addition to.' There is an element of exchange and substitution in it, except for one instance in Eph 5:31. Carson suggests 'instead of' is the best

---

[151] Barrett, *The Gospel According to St. John*, 29.

meaning for the preposition; he adds, "The grace and truth that came through Jesus Christ is what replaces the law."[152] So the limited grace that came from the Law was replaced by the grace and truth of the New Testament. This is further supported by the context of verse 17 which is linked with 16 by the conjunction ὅτι. In addition to the meaning of the preposition, the λόγος is identified by the person of Jesus Christ. Jesus is the source of ἡ χάρις καὶ ἡ ἀλήθεια (hē charis kai hē alētheia). In the context of Exodus 33-34, in verse 33:19, the Lord states that he will be gracious to whomever he will be gracious and merciful to whomever he will be merciful. יְהוָה (YHWH) is the source of all goodness as Jesus is the source of goodness in the New Testament.

---

[152] Carson, *The Gospel According to John*, 132.

God the Son

John 1:18 states that no one has seen θεός (actually θεόν since it is in the accusative case) but μονογενὴς θεός (monogenēs theos) who is at the Father's side has made him known. In order to provide convincing exegesis for this verse, the following question needs to be answered: Was God seen in the Old Testament. In Exod 33:20, Moses was told that he could not see the face of God and live. But Moses saw God from behind, not in his full glory. There is a sense in which not seeing God might imply that no one was able to see him in his full glory. There is another passage in Isa 6:5, in which Isaiah states that his eyes have seen the Lord. This passage is significant not just because Isaiah claims that he saw the Lord, but because the Gospel of John quotes from this passage in Isaiah. In John 12:39-41, it quotes from Isaiah 6 and it states that Isaiah spoke these words because he saw the glory of Jesus and spoke about him. The passage in Isaiah 6 speaks of Isaiah seeing the Lord in a very particular manner: Isaiah saw the Lord in his glory. Isa 6:3 states that the whole earth is full of the Lord's glory. In response to seeing the Lord and the glory of the Lord, Isaiah said, "Woe to me. I am ruined. For I am a man of unclean lips, and I live among a people of unclean lips, and my eyes have seen the King, the LORD Almighty." Whether John states that Isaiah saw the glory of Jesus or Jesus himself, the result is the same: Isaiah saw Jesus and his glory.[153] In particular, Isaiah saw not the incarnated Christ, but the μονογενὴς θεὸς ὁ ὢν εἰς τὸν κόλπον τοῦ πατρός (monogenēs theos ho ōn eis ton kolpon tou patros). There is truth to the claim that Isaiah probably could not see the full glory of the pre-incarnate God the Son; but the fact remains that he saw him.

The second question that needs to be answered is who is the θεός that no one has seen? Is the θεός a reference to God in general or does it refer to the Father or does it refer to the Son? If it refers to the Son, then the only way this verse can be understood is if it means that no one has seen the pre-incarnate Son in his full Glory. This is also true of the Father. This can be understood as, no one has seen God in his full Glory, but the incarnate Christ has made him known. This connects to John 1:14 where John states that he beheld his glory.[154] Several pieces of evidence suggest that while the last exegesis is true, there is an additional conclusion to be made.

First, John 6:46 states: not that anyone has seen the Father except he who is from God. The parallel between John 6:46 and John 1:18 suggests that the Son is the one who communicates the Father. Second, if the intention of John 1:18 is to only communicate the idea that the incarnation of Christ is how we are able to behold the full glory of God, then μονογενὴς θεός who is at the side of the Father is probably not the best way to express that idea. For John 1:18 does not highlight the incarnated Son, but emphasizes that θεός made θεός known. In other words, this verse is about God the Son communicating God the Father,

---

[153] White, *The Forgotten Trinity: Recovering the Heart of Christian Belief*, 137-138.
[154] Carson, *The Gospel According to John*, 134-135.

even before incarnation. Third, the pre-incarnate Son was seen and did reveal the Father before the incarnation and certainly revealed him more through the incarnation. It is evident that Isaiah saw the pre-incarnate Jesus and Moses saw the pre-incarnate Jesus in Exodus 33-34. As the Son has revealed some of the glory of God in the Old Testament, so he revealed and explained the Father better in the New Testament. It seems that the best meaning of the verse is that no one has seen God the Father, but God the Son has explained him. This does not negate the prior idea; instead, it supports it. But it also implies that when God appeared to the prophets of the Old Testament, it was God the Son, the λόγος, who appeared not God the Father.

In addition to that, John 1:18 provides a picture of a personal relationship between the λόγος and the Father. The author of the Gospel uses the following expression: μονογενὴς θεὸς ὁ ὢν εἰς τὸν κόλπον τοῦ πατρός. Carson states that this expression "apparently conveys an aura of intimacy, mutual love and knowledge."[155] The fact that the personhood is strongly attested to in the Prologue of John cannot be simply dismissed or overlooked for any parallelism in thought or allegory. Consider what Schnackenburg has to say about this:

If the exegesis of the prologue can be summarized in few words, there are five parameters that are emphasized, repeated, and carefully articulated in the Prologue of John, as well as the rest of the Gospel. These parameters are the fact that the λόγος is eternal, personal, God, creator, and has become flesh. When it comes to the theology of the Prologue of John, in particular the five parameters, the Old Testament fulfills all five. Furthermore, the Prologue of John has a strong dependence on

---

[155] Carson, *The Gospel According to John*, 135.

the theology, terminology, and imagery of the Old Testament. It echoes doctrines, images, and principles from it.

Philo

Philo's Background

Philo's writings deserve to be examined because they offer a personified λόγος that seems to be, in face value, similar to the one in the Prologue of John. There are two main tasks that are undertaken. First, a survey of key passages that can be taken as a background for the λόγος is undertaken. It is important to note that the overwhelming majority of scholars, proponents and opponents of Philo's writings as a background for the λόγος, utilize primarily one main thought; namely, the λόγος as the archetype and the agent of creation. The passages related to this thought will be discussed, but also all relevant passages from Philo will be investigated, even when the majority of modern scholars have not quoted or utilized them. There are two reasons for this approach. 1. There has been a resurrection of the hypothesis that Philo's writings are the background for the Prologue of John. This has been resurrected by some researchers, such as Dunn[156]. Although the majority of scholars do not follow this thought, there is anticipation that Philo might become an important area for research concerning the background of John. 2. This approach seeks first to constructs a philosophical system that acts as a hermeneutical framework or a lens. It would seem that interpreting various verses in the context of Philo's system better assists in determining their

---

[156] Dunn, *Christology in the Making*, 221-227.

meaning. This second task is an analysis and evaluation of Philo's background against the criteria that was set forth earlier is performed.

Philo tends to use the term λόγος in several ways. All occurrences of λόγος in Philo's writings have been examined and classified according to their intended meaning. The range of meaning of λόγος in Philo includes the following: divine Reason, words, matter, account, description, thing, Scripture, speech, and principle. The following pattern can be a helpful guide: the first term is ὀρθός λόγος, which means the right Reason. It is the general philosophical moral reason behind all logical principles, thoughts, and actions. It can refer to the archetype divine λόγος or it can be derived from it. The second term is θεῖος λόγος: the divine Reason. This is the most direct reference to the archetype λόγος, which Philo also defines as the image of God as will be demonstrated later. This is what Westcott has to say about it:

> When Philo speaks of "the divine Logos" his thought is predominantly of the divine Reason and not of the divine Word. This fact is of decisive importance. The conception of the divine Word, that is, of a divine will, sensibly manifested in personal action, is not naturally derived from that of a divine reason but is rather complementary to it, and a characteristic of different school of thought.[157]

It is interesting that Philo described the λόγος by using θεῖος and not θεο,ς, with one exception, which will be discussed later. Philo maintains clear separation and distinction between God and the λόγος. This fact will be significant in showing a major difference between the concepts of John and Philo. Third, ἱερὸς

---

[157] Westcott, *The Gospel According to St. John*, xvi.`

λόγος is the sacred word: the Scripture. In certain instances, the sacred Scriptures are an instance of the divine λόγος. This might point to the Jewish view of the Law in which the Law was created and preserved by God before it was written down. It still contains Platonic overtones that affected both worldviews. The fourth term is the λόγος θεοῦ: the word of God. This refers to the divine λόγος and sometimes, depending on the context, it can refer to Scripture. The fifth term is the προφητικὸς λόγος: the prophetical word; this refers to Scriptures. Often Philo can use the term λόγος to refer to all the above ideas.

Furthermore, the English translation sometimes utilizes the term reason to denote the same thing. In this book, the divine λόγος, Reason, divine Reason, and the λόγος will be mostly utilized to refer to the same thing unless explicitly stated otherwise.

The following is a survey of the most significant passages of Philo in relation to the λόγος. All passages in the Greek text of Philo's writings that contain the term λόγος were examined. The verses selected are the ones that shed light on the relationship between the λόγος and God, λόγος and creation, λόγος and light, λόγος and life, and λόγος and Wisdom. These passages are selected to explore every possible relationship between Philo and the Prologue of John.

Philo's system is a syncretistic one that combines Platonism, OT and possibly select elements of other Hellenistic thoughts. Therefore, Philo mixes the basic framework of Platonism with Old Testament, while attempting to maintain the fundamentals of Judaism. The gaps in Platonism are filled with his OT thoughts. The contradictions between the two systems, if resolved, favored one over the other.

Survey of Philo's Writings

Model and Archetype of the World

Philo states that when God created the physical universe, he created the world in two basic steps. It is similar to an architect of a city who first creates a model before the actual physical city is built. Therefore, God first created a mental or logical model. This logical model is the divine λόγος. Another way Philo describes it is that the logical model is contained in the divine λόγος. Philo states, "The universe that consisted of ideas would have no other location than the Divine Reason."[158] Whether it is the logical model, or it contains the logical model, both expressions really mean the same thing, for Philo utilizes them consistently in an interchangeable manner. The second step was that God used this model to create the world.[159] In another passage, Philo states that this model, or pattern, is the image of God which is the λόγος after which God fashioned the world.[160] In this reference, Philo uses just λόγος instead of θεῖος λόγος. This is because Philo sometimes utilizes the bare term λόγος to refer to θεῖος λόγος.

---

[158] Philo, *De Opificio Mundi*, 19-20.
[159] Philo, *De Opificio Mundi*, 19-20.
[160] Philo, *De Specialibus Legibus I*, 81.

In the philosophy of Philo, God is the architect. The architect created a model before he created the world. He fashioned the world according to the model. This model is the divine λόγος. Later Philo states that God is only one, and that he has no counselor. In other words, his understanding of the divine λόγος did not compromise his Jewish belief in the unity of God. He reiterates, "Now God, with no counselor to help Him (who was there beside him?)…"[161] This is important because there is one passage that might give the impression that Philo believes that the λόγος is a second deity. Nevertheless, Philo continues to advocate in his philosophical system that God is one and that the divine λόγος is only a created entity. Wolfson describes the λόγος in a multi-stage definition in which the mind of God is the λόγος, which thought out some patterns, or a model, or an archetype of the world. God then created an encasement or container to contain these models. Philo called this container the λόγος. The last stage is that the λόγος is the pattern itself or the totality of all ideas that form the model. [162] This is an unnecessary complex reading of the λόγος. Wolfson has been criticized for the multi-stage theory in that he attempted to make Philo more systematic than necessary. [163] The more direct explanation is that God created a large pattern for everything that he wanted to create. This big pattern is the λόγος. When Philo describes the model as the λόγος or as contained in the λόγος, in reality it means the same thing: the λόγος is the big pattern. What we see is Philo describing the same idea using different words and allegories.

---

[161] Philo, *De Opificio Mundi*, 23.
[162] Wolfson, *Philo*, 230-232.
[163] Darrell D. Hannah, *Michael and Christ: Michael Traditions and Angel Christology in Early Christianity* (Tübingen: Mohr Siebeck, 1999), 83.

To better demonstrate the idea of a container and the content of a container, Philo states that Moses named the divine λόγος 'the book,' referring to Gen 2:4. He states, "'Book' is Moses' name for the reason of God in which has been inscribed and engraved the formation of all else."[164] Philo did not say that the λόγος is actually a book. However, he calls the λόγος a book in that it contains the architecture of creation. Namely, a virtual book contains collections of architecture, ideas, and patterns. From examining the various symbolism and allegories, 'book' is a metaphor that Philo uses to describe the λόγος. What makes Philo's λόγος an attractive proposition is the fact that there are some allegories and symbols for the λόγος which give the impression of personification. However, in this case, the book is impersonal. Not all of the symbols and allegories are persons; some are impersonal entities. Wolfson explains:

> Everything in Scripture, from names, dates, and numbers to the narration of historical events or the prescription of rules from human conduct, is to him subject to allegorical interpretation.[165]

The symbolism never ends with Philo and for this reason, one must be careful in making bold determination when it comes to the personification of the λόγος.

Philo does not say that the λόγος is just the model for the physical world, but that man is fashioned according to that same model or archetype. Philo states that the image of God is the λόγος by which God utilized as a model to create humans.[166] Furthermore, the soul of man and the mind of man are fashioned

---

[164] Philo, *Legum Allegoriae I*, 19.
[165] Wolfson, *Philo*, 116.
[166] Philo, *De Opificio Mundi*, 25.

according to the λόγος: "For a man's soul is a precious thing, and when it departs to seek another home, all that will be left behind is defiled, deprived as it was of the divine image. This is because the mind of man has the form of God, being shaped in conformity with the ideal archetype, the Word that is above all."[167]

Philo has taken the metaphysical dualism of the two worlds of Plato and articulated its relationship to God. As in Platonism, there are two worlds, the material world and the nonmaterial world. The nonmaterial world contains the forms, the archetypes, and the perfect ideas. However, while Plato was not clear about his views about gods and their relationship to the metaphysical system, as articulated by Ronald Nash[168], Philo articulated the relationship between God and λόγος. God and λόγος are distinct. God is the creator of the λόγος. This is in contrast to Platonic system in which the forms or ideas are possibly eternal. But furthermore, Philo's interpretation of Platonism within his syncretism is in contrast of later Middle Platonism development in which God is associated with the highest form, the form of good.[169]

The Allegorical Methods of Philo

Philo brings in a foreign Greek concept and attempts to find biblical references to support his views.   Wolfson has the

---

[167] Philo, *De Specialibus Legibus III*, 207.
[168] Ronald H. Nash, *The Gospel and the Greeks* (Phillipsburg: P&R Publishing, 2003), 27-28.
[169] Nash, *The Gospel and the Greeks*, 44-45.

following to say about Philo's method of interpreting Scripture in light of Greek philosophies:

> It is Philo, however, who brought to full development this peculiar method of interpreting scripture and also this peculiar form of philosophic literature and it is to him that their vogue in the subsequent history of philosophy is to be traced.[170]

In order for Philo to accomplish his task of interpreting Scripture in the light of Greek philosophies, his utilization of scriptural references often seems manipulative of the text. This has been often asserted by scholars. For example, Wolfson states that the allegorical method is "made use of by Philo without any reservation."[171] Runia states, "Philo makes no attempt to present a systematic theory of knowledge."[172] Philo refers to the passage in Genesis where God created man according to his image and claims that the image of God is a separate entity from God. He says that man was not created according to the image of God but according to the image of the image of God.[173] Despite the fact that the passage in Genesis does not state or imply that God created a second entity called the image of God and then created man according to the image of that image, Philo reads this meaning from this passage. This suggests that Philo' readings of this passage is to find support for a Hellenistic philosophical concept, even when the context of the Scriptural passage does not support it. It is imperative not to carry the

---

[170] Wolfson, *Philo*, 95.
[171] Wolfson, *Philo*, 116.
[172] Runia, "Philo of Alexandria," in *Routledge Encyclopedia of Philosophy*, 358.
[173] Philo, *De Opificio Mundi*, 25.

grammatical and linguistic arguments of Philo to other Greek writings. Wolfson states the following about this:

> There is a variety and mixture of vocabulary in the presentation of his philosophy, and there is no attempt to adhere to the technical vocabulary of the schools or to one consistent technical set of terms of one school.[174]

For example, in De Somniis, 227-230, Philo finds a passage in the LXX that mentions θεός twice: one with an article and one without. The reason that this passage has two occurrences is because it translates the Hebrew name Bethel literally to τόπῳ θεοῦ. Philo states that this passage gives an indication that there might be two gods. However, he claims that the divine λόγος is referred to by θεός without the article and that this does not contradict his Jewish monotheism, because in that verse ὁ θεός refers to the One God.

This is the only instance in which he calls λόγος by the title θεός. James Dunn, Kenneth Schenck,[175] Gregory Sterling,[176] and David Runia make a link to John 1:1c.[177] The link is that John utilized Philo's rhetoric in his Prologue. However, in John 20:28, an articular θεός was applied to Jesus. As has been demonstrated, John has applied both articular and anarthrous θεός to the Father and the Son. Furthermore, an anarthrous θεός can also be definite as this author proposes about John 1:1c; and

---

[174] Wolfson, *Philo*, 97.
[175] Kenneth Schenck, *A Brief Guide to Philo* (Louisville: John Knox Press, 2005), 88.
[176] Gregory E. Sterling, "The Place of Philo of Alexandria in the Study of Christian Origins," in *Philo und das Neue Testament,* ed. Roland Deines and Karl-Wilhelm Niebuhr (Tübingen: Mohr Siebeck, 2004), 48.
[177] David T. Runia, *Philo in Early Christian Literature: A Survey* (Assen: Van Gorcum, 1993), 83.

even if it is not, a qualitative θεός of John 1:1c carries the same weight of full deity as a definite one. Therefore, this strange anomaly should only be attributed to Philo's own methodologies. To be fair to Runia, he states the following:

> In conclusion, it must be said that, in spite of the studies we have cited, the consensus of Johannine scholarship adopts a very cautious approach to the subject of the relation between Philo and John.[178]

What Philo does with the image of God and with θεός, he does repeatedly with other entities. The following is another reference by Philo in which he compares the λόγος to the shadow of God. He uses Bezalel, the name of a person in the book of Exodus, as an allegory to the λόγος. Philo takes the meaning of Bezalel, in the shadow of God, and applies it to the λόγος. In that reference, in which the name of Bezalel is an allegory to the λόγος, he demonstrates again his idea of the image of God:

> For just as God is the pattern of the image, to which the title of shadow has just been given, even so the image becomes the pattern of other beings, as the prophet made clear ... by saying, "and God made the man after the image of God" (Gen i.27), implying that the image had been made such as representing God, but that the man was made after the image when it had acquired the force of a pattern.[179]

Therefore, it is important not to confuse the created immaterial pattern or archetype with the various titles and labels which Philo assigns to the pattern. Furthermore, the shadow of God does not imply a divine part of God, but a created entity serving

---

[178] Runia, *Philo in Early Christian Literature: A Survey*, 83.
[179] Philo, *Legum Allegoriae III*, 95-96.

as a pattern for the rest of creation. At the same time, the term shadow brings to mind Plato's cave. However, there is a significant difference: For Plato, there are two principles, for Philo, there are three: God, the image, and then all created things, each the shadow of the other.

The Divine λόγος as a Created Entity and not the Architect

Philo states that the λόγος originated by God, and that God is not a partaker of it. It is a separate entity of God which was created by him, "Of the power of vitality the irrational creatures partake with us; of the power of reasoning God is, not indeed partaker, but originator, being the fountain of archetypal Reason." [180] In the above reference, the λόγος is the archetypal Reason: τοῦ πρεσβυτάτου λόγου. That phrase can be translated as 'the most ancient Reason.' It sets the relationship between God and the λόγος. Wolfson affirms that in Philo's example of the architect,[181] the λόγος is created by God as a real entity outside of the essence of God.[182]

This is significant because often the λόγος is described by various authors, such as Dunn[183] and Sterling,[184] as the agent of and participant in creation with God. For example, Runia alludes to that by stating that the λόγος is the agent of creation and the

---

[180] Philo, *Quod Deterius Potiori Insidiari Soleat*, 82.
[181] Philo, *De Opificio Mundi*, 20.
[182] Wolfson, *Philo*, 245.
[183] Dunn, *Christology in the Making*, 221-227.
[184] Sterling, "The Place of Philo of Alexandria in the Study of Christian Origins," in *Philo und das Neue Testament*,49.

architect.[185] Wolfson, however, insists that the architect is God and not the λόγος.[186] Wolfson also explains how the λόγος is the instrument or agent of God in creation: It is not that God delegated the work of creation to the λόγος, but that God created the world directly. The sense here is that, "the λόγος is to be called the instrument only in the sense that it is through the intelligible world as a pattern, with which λόγος is identical, that the visible world was created."[187] This is in contrast to Stoicism in which the λόγος is seen as an active agent. For concerning Philo, λόγος is at best a passive created entity for the use of Architect. This might suggest that Stoicism has less role to play in the λόγος of Philo as was previously thought.

The Relationship between λόγος and God

Philo makes the following statement about the λόγος that can be possibly understood to imply that the λόγος is part of God. However, this is not a typical or repeated claim of Philo:

> The voice told me that while God is indeed one, his highest and chiefest powers are two, even goodness and sovereignty. Through his goodness he begat all that is, through his sovereignty He rules what he has begotten. And in the midst between the two there is a third which unites them, Reason, for it is through reason that God is both ruler and good.[188]

There is an apparent contradiction in Philo's argument. He sees Reason as part of God; nevertheless, Reason was

---

[185] David T. Runia, *Philo of Alexandria and the Timaeus of Plato* (Leiden: E. J. Brill, 1986), 447.
[186] Wolfson, *Philo*, 244.
[187] Wolfson, *Philo*, 270.
[188] Philo, *De Cherubim*, 27.

conceived, as the above passage later states[189]; but if Reason was not eternal because it was conceived at certain point of time and if Reason was part of God, then this would imply that God is not eternal. Philo sees the need for an entity that is part of God, i.e., Reason. God needs Reason; and Reason is needed for everything else. Therefore, it must have been created or conceived before everything else. At the same time, in this passage, Philo does not attribute creation as a function of Reason. Furthermore, there is a possible hint of Platonic form, in particular the form of good.[190] Does Philo view some of the higher Platonic forms as attributes of God? The point is that Philo does not seem to provide a systematic interpretation of the OT, nor is the OT the whole source of his worldview. In conclusion, although the above passage may be taken to say that Reason is part of God, it is not a typical statement of Philo. Whatever the meaning of this passage is, it is probably best be understood from the following the context, "God is, not indeed partaker, but originator, being the fountain of archetypal Reason."[191] Many have observed that Philo lacks consistency with his theology and philosophy.[192] The inconsistency is unavoidable due to syncretism. However, there is a pattern in Philo that highlights the relationship between God and λόγος: In Philo, God is the exclusive creator, maker, craftsman, father, cause, and planter. Philo applies these terms exclusively to God.[193]

---

[189] Philo, *De Cherubim*, 27.
[190] Nash, *The Gospel and the Greeks*, 25.
[191] Philo, *Quod Deterius Potiori Insidiari Soleat*, 82.
[192] Nash, *The Gospel and the Greeks*, 73.
[193] Wolfson, *Philo*, 211.

Philo's Dualism: Physical and Incorporeal

Philo states, "The incorporeal world, then, was now finished and firmly settled in the Divine reason, and the world patent to sense was ripe for birth after the pattern of the incorporeal."[194] In the above reference, Philo explains the process of creation. The first part is the creation of the incorporeal world that is contained in the divine λόγος. When the first part was completed, God proceeded to create the physical world from the incorporeal model. According to Philo, the divine λόγος is not physical. It is an incorporeal collection of ideas, patterns, and models, which must be created first before the creation of the physical world. The world, including humans, is the physical instance of the divine λόγος. Philo reiterates this with more accuracy:

> Let no one represent the likeness as one to a bodily form; for neither is God in human form, nor is the human body God-like. No, it is in respect of the Mind, the sovereign element of the soul, that the word "image" is used; for after the pattern of a single Mind, even the mind of the Universe as an archetype, the mind in each of those who successively came into being was molded. [195]

In the above reference, Philo comments on the relationship between the image of God and creation and the fact that the Bible states that man was created in the image of God. The image of God is the divine λόγος. Furthermore, Philo states earlier that the world was created according to the incorporeal pattern that is, or is contained, in the divine λόγος. In the above

---

[194] Philo, *De Opificio Mundi*, 36.
[195] Philo, *De Opificio Mundi*, 69.

passage, Philo explains the relationship of an entity that was created in the image or likeness of another entity: it is not that the original entity is physical, but instead the physical entity is according to the pattern of an incorporeal entity. In other words, as the physical world was created according to the pattern of the divine λόγος, no one should assume that the λόγος is physical, in the same way that God is not physical.

Here we see a dualistic system. One world is physical and the other is not. The physical world is created according to the immaterial divine λόγος. Furthermore, the immaterial model is superior to the physical instance and is closer to God. For example, concerning the plural expression, "let us make man in our own image" in Genesis, Philo suggests that angels were involved in the creation of man since God cannot be responsible for the creation of evil. However, he does not insist on it: "The full truth about cause of this it must needs be that God alone knows…"[196] This is an important development over Platonism in the association of good and evil with the two worlds.[197] However, it is important to note that while this passage allows for angels to be agent of creation in contradiction of OT and in contradiction of Philo's system, nowhere λόγος is given that role.

Up to this point, Philo draws from the Genesis text of creation and his Greek philosophy to paint a picture of the relationship between God and creation. He sees the importance of the divine λόγος in the creation of the world, being an immaterial model of the world, but he does not come to the correct understanding of the text. He supplies his commentary

[196]Philo, *De Opificio Mundi*, 73.
[197] Nash, *The Gospel and the Greeks*, 32-33.

with Greek philosophy. Wolfson makes a point when he discusses Philo's approach about creation. He suggests that some of the ideas, concerning the pre-creation of an entity as a model for a physical entity, are a combination of Jewish tradition with Platonic theory of ideas. For example, God created an ideal pattern of the tabernacle before creating the world. This is a model for the physical tabernacle.[198]

Philo discusses the relationship of humans with the λόγος. He states that the mind of every man is allied to the divine λόγος since it is a copy of it. At the same time, the physical body of the man is allied to the world.[199] Philo describes the divine λόγος as the mind or soul of God. All humans have a mind that is a fragment or copy of the original archetype. The Greek dualism is very clear in the above reference. Such dualism is not seen in John. This dualism can also be illustrated in another way:

> This is as much as to say that God ceases molding the masses that are mortal, whenever he begins to make those that are divine and in keeping with the nature of seven…, whenever there comes upon the soul the holy Reason of which Seven in the keynote, six together with all mortal things that the soul seems to make therewith comes to a stop.[200]

In this illustration, Philo describes the work of God and the rest of God. In the mind of Philo, there are dualistic system: the mortal physical world and the incorporeal world. There are also two kinds of work for God: God's creation of the physical world, and God's creation of the incorporeal world. When God rested from all his works, he rested from all of his activities which were

---

[198] Wolfson, *Philo,* 182.
[199] Philo, *De Opificio Mundi,* 146.
[200] Philo, *Legum Allegoriae I,* 16-17.

related to the creation of the physical mortal world. According to Philo, this mortal physical work is denoted by the number 6. When God stopped all mortal activities, he worked on the incorporeal realm which is also the divine realm. The λόγος belongs to that divine incorporeal realm. Moreover, Philo defined the interaction of the λόγος with the soul as belonging to that incorporeal realm that starts when the mortal physical world halts. The dualism here is that God organizes his creation into two spheres: immortal and mortal.

Philo describes the importance of understanding the physical world and the λόγος. According to Philo, the mind of a man is allied to the λόγος, and through the mind, a person can understand the λόγος since he was created according to the pattern of the λόγος. This is how God is understood as well. God is in the incorporeal realm and the mind is the connection to the divine incorporeal realm.[201] Experiencing the λόγος is not a personal experience with a personal λόγος, but a mental experience beyond the physical world. This is also demonstrated in the following reference, which discusses the need for the body to achieve what the soul is made of. In particular, it is the need of the body to attain salvation, as a natural consequence of the soul's creation in accordance to the archetype λόγος:

> It followed then, as a natural consequence of man's soul having been made after the image of the archetype, the Word of the First cause, that his body also was made erect, and could lift up its eyes to heaven, the purest portion of our universe that by means of that which he could see man might clearly apprehend that which he could not see.[202]

---

[201] Philo, *Legum Allegoriae III*, 100.
[202] Philo, *De Plantatione*, 20.

Philo further explains the experience of God in terms of manna. Philo argues that manna means something generic, and thus it is a befitting allegory for the λόγος of God, since it is above the physical world and was created before all created things. [203] Moreover, Philo explains the role of manna in experiencing God:

> But Jacob, looking even higher than the word, says that he is fed by God Himself... He looks on God as feeding him, not his word; but the Angel, who is the word, as healer of ills. This is the language of a true philosopher. [204]

Philo does not imply that the λόγος is either an angel or a person. However, Philo sees various names, words, persons, things, and passages to be symbolic or allegorical to the λόγος.

Nash summarizes Plato's dualism in three categories: metaphysical dualism as seen in the "distinction between two worlds," epistemological dualism as seen in the "distinction between sense experience and reason" and in that "sense experience always falls short of producing knowledge," and anthropological dualism in the "radical distinction between body and soul."[205] All of these categories are articulated by Philo for his system. For Plato's dualism, the heart of it is the world of forms which corresponds to λόγος in Philo. As a Platonic philosopher, Philo is highly concerned with Reason and with feeding on Reason; hence it is the focal point of his writings. Therefore, he sees every passage in light of philosophical Reason. At the same time, he keeps his allegiance to his Judaism

---

[203] Philo, *Legum Allegoriae III*, 175.
[204] Philo, *Legum Allegoriae III*, 177.
[205] Nash, *The Gospel and the Greeks*, 29-30.

by stating that God is higher than Reason and that he should be sought directly.

σοφία and λόγος

The relationship between σοφία (sophia, wisdom) and λόγος in Philo's writings is not as expected. Σοφία is not the same as λόγος[206] but they are related to each other. Both are created entities. Philo states, "but of him whose is σοφία itself also, even God who created it and makes it his."[207] Verses that suggest that the λόγος is the same or distinct from σοφία will be examined. One verse that might suggest some relationship between them is when Philo compares the λόγος to gold, "And so reason, which is more precious than gold, the rich and manifold union of myriad forms, is brought to its excellent perfection."[208]

This might be relevant since Proverbs 8 compares σοφία to gold. That parallelism does not imply that Philo derived it from Proverbs 8. Nevertheless, this statement is noted.

Furthermore, σοφία is seen as the agent of creation, and is also seen as a Mother, "If you accord a father's honor, to him who created the world, and a mother's honor to wisdom, by whose agency the universe was brought to completion, you will yourself be the gainer."[209] In the above reference, Philo confuses the agency of creation. In an earlier text, Philo claimed that the goodness of God is the agent of creation. What did God utilize

---

[206] Philo, *Legum Allegoriae II*, 86.
[207] Philo, *Legum Allegoriae I*, 77.
[208] Philo, *De Sacrificiis Abelis Et Caini*, 83.
[209] Philo, *Quod Deterius Potiori Insidiari Soleat*, 54.

for the creation of the world? Is it λόγος or σοφία? From Philo's perspective, it does not matter. It can be both. As God utilized one element, he can utilize another. All of them are created, impersonal tools in the process of creation. While this suggests that Philo was probably not afraid of honoring a female entity, and that he had strong regard for Mother σοφία; at the same time, he did not see her to be the same as λόγος. This might not work well for the proponent of the idea that Philo was at least the linguistic link between the female σοφία and the male λόγος.

Wolfson suggests that λόγος and σοφία are the same; he does not see problems in the texts that distinguish σοφία from λόγος.[210] He offers a complex explanation that λόγος is used in a multi-stage definition hypothesis. As has been seen earlier, the meaning of the λόγος is changed in each stage. So the distinction between σοφία and λόγος is actually a distinction from the λόγος in one of those stages.[211] Wolfson offers a complex systematic solution to solve the inconsistent usages and the constant systematic philosophical problems of Philo.[212] A better and easier solution than Wolfson's complex multi-stage definition hypothesis is that σοφία is distinct from λόγος, even when they sometimes share allegories, descriptions, and functions. However, at the least, there is some interaction and close relationship between the λόγος and σοφία, as much as, there are such relationships and interactions between the various attributes, "powers", actions, and descriptions of God and men and the λόγος.

---

[210] Wolfson, *Philo*, 261.
[211] Wolfson, *Philo*, 260.
[212] Hannah, *Michael and Christ*, 77.

Darrell Hannah proposes another direction. He suggests parallels between Philo and the Wisdom of Solomon and proposes that this could be the link; especially when he claims that both writings were dependent on Platonic ideas.[213] He proposes that Philo was familiar directly or indirectly with the Wisdom of Solomon and its identification of σοφία with λόγος.[214] This is an interesting hypothesis. However, the real test is within the writings of Philo. As stated before, Philo explicitly distinguishes between λόγος and σοφία.

Schenck follows Tobin by stating that in spite of the fact that OT wisdom imagery, with the rest of wisdom literature, offer much to illuminate the Prologue of John, they "do not account for all imagery" in the Prologue, and more importantly, they do not offer the shift to the term λόγος from σοφία. He suggests that Philo is the link;[215] but this is a sword of two edges. It is true that the second temple wisdom background is similar to Philo's concept of λόγος as Wolfson repeatedly asserted;[216] however, if Philo's λόγος concept fails to meet the criteria, then the wisdom literature fails as well. On the other hand, if the link does not exist, the connection to the Gospel of John is severed. Therefore, in either case, whether hypothetically σοφία is the same as λόγος in Philo or not, this will not affect the book's conclusion. It will be demonstrated later that the concepts in both Philo and later wisdom writings are not compatible with the Prologue of John. However, the later wisdom books need that linguistic connection.

---

[213] Hannah, *Michael and Christ*, 91.
[214] Hannah, *Michael and Christ*, 81.
[215] Schenck, *A Brief Guide to Philo*, 87.
[216] Wolfson, *Philo*, 287.

λόγος is not Eternal.

The Prime Position of λόγος

In the following reference, Philo demonstrates that no one was with God:

> It may mean that neither before creation was there anything with God, nor, when the universe had come into being, does anything take its place with him; for there is absolutely nothing which he needs. A yet better interpretation is the following. God is alone, a Unity, in the sense that his nature is simple not composite whereas each one of us of all other created beings is made up of many things.[217]

The closest that Philo comes to the idea that the λόγος is with God is when he states the following: "But the primal existence is God, and next to him is the Word of God, but all other things subsist in word only, but in their active effects they are in some cases as good as none-subsisting."[218] This is important because having a philosophical or religious entity beside or close to God has always been suggested as a possible link to the λόγος of John. Philo places high value on the Word of God. However, in Philo's own system, it is a created entity and therefore it is not eternal. On this, Wolfson asserts, "God from eternity was alone and anything else besides Him must have been brought into being by God through an act of creation."[219] Therefore, that passage refers not to eternal existence but prime existence. It seems that Philo ascribes honor to the symbol of Greek philosophy, and at the same time, he honors his Jewish

---

[217] Philo, *Legum Allegoriae II*, 2.
[218] Philo, *Legum Allegoriae II*, 86.
[219] Wolfson, *Philo*, 201.

monotheism. The meaning of the prime position next to God is best explained in that the divine λόγος is the first created entity, and therefore, it deserves the highest honor after God:

> We have a proof of this in His feeding us with his own most "generic" word; for "manna" means "something," and this is the most generic of all terms. And the word of God is above all the world, and is eldest and most all-embracing of created things.[220]

In showing that the prime position of the λόγος is toward God, Philo takes Reason or λόγος as the eldest of God in that it was the first created entity. Schenck sees in this a possible link to John.[221] Nevertheless, this has absolutely nothing to do with the New Testament definition of sonship; for the sonship in the NT is based on eternal loving relationship between the Father and the Son, and not that the Son was the first created impersonal entity. Nevertheless, this passage is consistent with all other passages in which Philo makes Reason or λόγος to be the center of OT passages. In other words, Philo wants to place the divine Reason at the most prime position:

> It is Reason, who has taken refuge with God and become his suppliant, that is here given the name Levite. This Reason God took from the midst and most sovereign part of the soul, that is he drew it and allotted to himself and adjudged to it that portion of the eldest son. And this it is clear from this that, while Reuben was the first-born of Jacob, Levi is the first-born of Israel.[222]

---

[220] Philo, *Legum Allegoriae III*, 175.

[221] Schenck, *A Brief Guide to Philo*, 89.

[222] Philo, *De Sacrificiis Abelis Et Caini*, 118.

In all of the references in which Philo assigns some sort of prime position to λόγος, he always maintains the superiority of God, as Wolfson asserts, "The superiority of God to the ideas consists, according to Philo, in the fact that He is their creator."[223] The superiority of God is illustrated in the following example in which Philo asserts that Reason is the High Priest and has limited access to the presence of God, "Mark you that not even the high-priest Reason, though has the power to dwell in unbroken leisure amid the scared doctrines, has received free license to resort to them at every season, but barely once a year (Lev. Xvi.2, 34)."[224] Philo attempts to find a place for Reason in every passage of the Old Testament even when it is not mentioned; as he tries to find a place for the Greek λόγος in his monotheistic Jewish faith. Allegory is the syncretistic tool that he utilizes to bridge this gap.

What should be made of Philo's description of the λόγος as eternal? Philo states that it is eternal in two references. The first reference is, "…and that the everlasting Word of the eternal God is the very sure and staunch prop of the whole."[225] In the second reference, Philo states the following:

> Now while others, by asserting that our human mind is a particle of the ethereal substance, have claimed for man a kinship with the upper air; our great Moses likened the fashion of the reasonable soul to no created thing, but averred it to be a genuine coinage of that read Spirit, the Divine and Invisible One, signed and impressed by the seal of God, the stamp of which is the Eternal Word.[226]

---

[223] Wolfson, *Philo*, 204.
[224] Philo, *De Gigantibus*, 52.
[225] Philo, *De Plantatione*, 8.
[226] Philo, *De Plantatione*, 18.

Sterling suggests that Philo's description of the λόγος as eternal might provide a link to the Prologue of John. [227] Nevertheless, the context of this attribute does not imply that the λόγος never had an origin. In all of these instances, the Greek term ἀίδιος can be translated as either 'eternal' or 'everlasting.' It should probably be translated 'everlasting,' since the context of Philo suggests that the λόγος had an origin. Wolfson states the following, "Indeed in two passages he does use the term eternal in connection with the term idea, but...it may only mean 'everlasting', that is indestructible."[228] Wolfson's assertion is supported by the following reference from Philo, "A statute which is law in the true sense is thereby eternal, since right reason, which is identical with law is not destructible." [229]

In fact, in the various references that the word ἀίδιος was used, when it is used about humans or created entities, the context makes it clear that the intention is everlasting. For example, in one of the references, Philo talks about the ἀίδιος life for the pious humans and the ἀίδιος death for the impious humans.[230] In another reference, Philo contrasts two worlds, one world is ἀίδιος and the other world is φθαρτός: perishable.[231] Wolfson states that the λόγος in Philo's writings was never uncreated and "had no eternal existence even in the mind of God; it was conceived by God only when he decided to create the world."[232] This is a fair and correct summary for the intention of Philo, and it reflects exactly to the spirit of the writings.

---

[227] Sterling, "The Place of Philo of Alexandria in the Study of Christian Origins," in *Philo und das Neue Testament*,48.
[228] Wolfson, *Philo*, 209.
[229] Philo, *De Ebrietate*, 142.
[230] Philo, *De Posteritate Caini*, 39.
[231] Philo, *De Aeternitate Mundi*, 9.
[232] Wolfson, *Philo*, 228.

Relationship between Light and λόγος

The Prologue of John establishes a particular relationship between light and the λόγος. Therefore, it is understandable to investigate whether there is the same kind of relationship between the λόγος of Philo and light. Schenck and Sterling[233] suggest that the fact that light is connected with the λόγος means that there can be a possible link.[234] The link is qualified by Schenck, however, in that he sees that Philo's concept of light is Platonic in nature while there are no platonic overtones in John. The following is the best passage that might demonstrate the light connection from Philo:

> Accordingly they are steadied by Aaron, the Word, and Hor, which is "light"; and life has no clearer light than truth. The prophet's aim therefore is to show thee by means of symbols that the doings of the wise man are upheld by the most essential of all things, the word and truth.[235]

In the above reference, Philo uses light, life, and λόγος in the same sentence. However, it falls short from the true understanding of John. Philo states that Hor is a symbol of light; and light is a symbol of truth. He associates the λόγος with Aaron, and concludes that the aim of the λόγος is truth. This seems to be a word play on the Hebrew word אור which means light. But for John, life is found in λόγος and that life is the source of light. This is completely different from Philo's worldview. Wolfson provides another difference. He states that

---

[233] Sterling, "The Place of Philo of Alexandria in the Study of Christian Origins," in *Philo und das Neue Testament,* 50.
[234] Schenck, *A Brief Guide to Philo,* 89.
[235] Philo, *Legum Allegoriae III,* 45.

while the λόγος is connected to light in Philo, this must be seen in the context that Philo ascribes the attribute 'lightgiver' to God.[236] In other words, in Philo's writings, the λόγος is not the source of light. This is in contrast to the λόγος in John. For example, John 5:26 states that as God has life in himself, so he granted the Son to have life in himself. This verse might suggest that the Father is the source of life of the Son. However, that verse needs to be interpreted in the context that the Son was eternal. There was no point of time that he did not exist. Therefore, the act of granting the Son to have life in himself is understood from that context. Carson suggests, "The impartation of life-in-himself to the Son must be an act belonging to eternity, of a piece with the eternal Father/Son relationship, which is itself of a piece with the relationship between the Word and God, a relationship that existed 'in the beginning'."[237] However, there is nothing in this verse that suggests that this is an eternal impartation or an eternal event. Moreover, John Feinberg states, "It is hard to know what this means other than that God depends on no one but himself for his life."[238] If the Divine Son was granted life in himself, he could not have been eternal. The author suggests that the best explanation for this verse is the incarnation.[239] Verses 26-27 are the response of Christ to the religious leaders concerning his deity and how the right to judge in verses 22-25: How can a mere man be God? Why would God give a man the right to judge and thus be honored as God? The Father -as a representative of the Triune God and therefore what applies to the Father applies to the Son and the Holy Spirit- has

---

[236] Wolfson, *Philo*, 211.

[237] Carson, *The Gospel According to John*, 257.

[238] John Feinberg, *No One Like Him* (Wheaton: Crossway Books, 2001), 212.

[239] John Calvin, *John* (Wheaton: Crossway Books, 1994), 133.

life in himself, so he granted for the Son to exist as human, having an additional human nature. In other words, God can acquire a second nature and can become a man. There is nothing that God cannot do, and that includes the incarnation. But it was not the Father who incarnated, it was the Son that was. Not that Son became the Son in incarnation. Before the incarnation, the Father and the Son always existed in eternal relationship. They always had life in themselves within the one Triune essence. The incarnation was the event that granted the Son to have life as a human outside the Father, in that only the Son incarnated and not the Father. As the eternal Divine Son, he always had life in him and always existed in eternal relationship with the Father. The context of this verse supports this interpretation. For verse 27 is exact parallel to verse 26. In verse 27, the Father has granted the incarnated Son, being the perfect man, the authority to judge precisely ὅτι υἱὸς ἀνθρώπου ἐστίν (hoti huios anthrōpou estin, because he is the son of man). υἱὸς ἀνθρώπου ἐστίν stands in parallel to verse 26. And καὶ ἐξουσίαν ἔδωκεν αὐτῷ καὶ κρίσιν ποιεῖν (kai exousian edōken autō kai krisin poiein) stands in parallel to verse 25. So as verse 26 gives the reason to 25, so verse 27b gives reason to 27a. And the reason in both cases is the incarnation of the Son of God.

The λόγος as an Agent of Reason and Principle of Correctness

Philo comments on the biblical narration of Hagar's encounter with the angel of the Lord. He states that the armed angel is the λόγος of God.[240] In a second reference to Exodus, he makes the same connection.[241] The first passage is a reference to Hagar and the Angel of the Lord. Philo automatically refers to the Angel of the Lord as the divine λόγος. To Hannah, this is significant; he proposes that the 'powers' of God are actually angels and that the λόγος is an actual archangel. This is part of his quest to find connections between Michael the archangel's speculation and Philo.[242] Nevertheless, this does not imply that Philo views the λόγος as a person or as God, but that he views persons, characters, names, items, and descriptions as allegorical to philosophical and moral concepts. Philo does not suggest that the λόγος will be carried by an angel, nor will be a specific event in which the λόγος will visit the world. But in the normal way of living, God has appointed Reason to be the guide that shows the way to people. It is a humanistic understanding of scripture that is devoid of prophecy, personal relationship, and miracle. On the other extreme, correct geometrical figures or angles are symbols of Reason. This demonstrates that the λόγος, in the mind of Philo, is a concept at best: "Right angles are clear pictures of rightness of reasoned thought, and right reason is an ever flowing spring of virtue."[243] It is noteworthy to point out Nash's explanation that numbers, correct geometrical figures and many other classes are part of the Platonic world of forms.[244]

Moreover, Hannah cautions about drawing strong conclusions regarding that connection since Philo's description of the λόγος is closer to Platonic ideas than the speculations of

---

[240] Philo, *De Cherubim*, 35.
[241] Philo, *De Agricultura*, 51.
[242] Hannah, *Michael and Christ*, 85.
[243] Philo, *De Plantatione*, 121.
[244] Nash, *The Gospel and the Greeks*, 25.

Michael since the concepts of λόγος and Michael are different.[245] Philo portrays the Angel of the Lord as nothing more than the voice of the impersonal divine λόγος. To him, the Angel is only logical advice, so that people will take the correct reasonable action that God wants them to take.

For example, Philo states, "If you had learned from the first that is not your life pursuits which bring your share in good or ill, but the divine Reason, the ruler and steersman of all, you should bear with more patience what befalls you." [246] In this, Philo associates goodness and accuracy with Reason. To him, Reason is what prompts a person to make right and correct choices. As Philo utilized the angel of the Lord and the correct geometrical angles as allegories to the λόγος denoting the correctness and rightness of reasoned thought, he does the same with Eden. In the following reference, Eden is a symbol of the divine λόγος, "'Eden' is a symbolic name for right and divine reason."[247]

Relationship between Scripture and λόγος

In the following reference, Philo implies that the λόγος and the writings of scripture are the same, at least in this context. Furthermore, 'Genuine philosophy' agrees with scripture:

---

[245] Hannah, *Michael and Christ*, 90.
[246] Philo, *De Cherubim*, 36.
[247] Philo, *De Posteritate Caini*, 32.

This royal road then, which we have just said to be true and genuine philosophy, is called in the law the utterance and word (λόγος) of God, for it is written, "thou shalt not swerve aside from the word which I command thee this day to the right hand nor to the left hand" (deu xxviii. 14). Thus it is clearly proved that the word of God is identical with the royal road.[248]

Philo states the same thing in a different context: "A statute which is law in the true sense is thereby eternal, since right reason, which is identical with law, is not destructible."[249]

In another passage, Philo states, "Yet deny that right reason, which is the fountain head of all other law."[250] Either the λόγος is the same as the law, as one passage affirms, or the λόγος is the source or fountain of the law. The true meaning, in the mind of Philo, seems that divine Reason is the archetype of the law. If the λόγος is the archetype of every physical entity created by God, then it can be seen as the archetype of the law. If it is the archetype of the law, then it is the fountain of the law. If the law was written according to the thoughts, ideas, and patterns of the λόγος , then it is seen in a certain sense to be the same as the λόγος . No wonder Philo refers to the λόγος as the book.[251] Reason is an ultimate path to living because it is the ultimate archetype and pattern which is the foundation for everything. This explains the strong affinity of the λόγος to scriptures and the Law; not just the Jewish Law, but all other laws which urge their followers to walk in the right way: in reason.

---

[248] Philo, *De Posteritate Caini*, 102.
[249] Philo, *De Ebrietate*, 142.
[250] Philo, *Quod Omnis Probus Liber Sit*, 47.
[251] Philo, *Legum Allegoriae I*, 19.

Evaluation of Philo's System

Summary of Philo's Concept of the λόγος

The concept of the λόγος in Philo's writings can be summarized as follows: before God created the world and created the Law, God created an archetype Reason. This Reason is perfect and existed before everything and yet it was created. It was the archetype for all humans, for the world and for the law. God created the world according to that archetype which he calls his image. This is parallel to Plato's world of forms, the heart of Philo's philosophical framework. Philo's system is not identical to the Platonic forms, for Philo specified the relationship between his Jewish God and the forms. In particular, God is not the forms or one of the forms, God is the architect of the reason. This thought is missing in Platonism and is only relevant in the context of Judaism. While the syncretism of Philo might seem successful at face value, it contains ample of gaps, contradictions, inconsistencies, and compromises.

Philo's writings consist of reading his syncretistic system in of the Old Testament. For example, where it states in the book of Genesis that God created man according to his own image, Philo asserts that the 'image' is an actual created entity. So according to Philo, God created two entities: man and the image of God. This led Philo to use the expression "the image of an image." Such massaging of the text to fit it into his worldview is the normative practice of Philo due to syncretism. Philo inserts the divine Reason in numerous passages of the Old Testament. The divine Reason is the archetype of many elements: the mind of man, the soul of man, the physical man, the physical world, and the Law of Moses.

The archetype Reason is an impersonal entity. It is not eternal, and has limited access to God. The divine Reason is not Wisdom, but works with her, as he works with other powers of God, such as goodness and supremacy. The divine Reason is related to morality. In the mind of Philo, doing the "reasonable" thing is also doing the moral thing. Morality and Reason go hand in hand. If someone seeks to do the right thing, then he must use his mind to guide him to sound reason. That sound reason is derived from the divine Reason, the archetype that was first created. Philo looks at the Old Testament and he sees every passage from the perspective of Reason. The moral, reasonable character is a symbol of Reason. It is befitting for every man to follow Reason. Thus, Philo views the following as symbolic to Reason: the angel of the Lord, the chief priest, various OT personalities, names, numbers, and other things. To Philo, Reason is the central theme of the Old Testament. Philo maintains a clear separation between the immaterial and physical worlds. The immaterial world is good while the physical world is corrupt. Divine Reason is perfect because it only operates within the good, immaterial world. A human being connects to divine Reason through his mind, which was created according to the image of Reason.

Observations from Scholars

The following are some observations by Scholars regarding Philo's λόγος:

First, the essence of Philo's λόγος is Hellenistic Platonic philosophy. This conclusion is supported universally by many such as Hannah,[252] Dunn,[253] Adam Kamesar,[254] Thomas Tobin,[255] Westcott,[256] Runia[257],Nash[258] and Schenck[259]. Wolfson states, "Philo is thus a critic of Stoicism and a reviser of Platonism."[260]

Second, John is not influenced by any Greek philosophy. Elizabeth Harris sees no possible way in which Stoicism has a direct influence on the Gospel of John.[261] Hurtado asserts, "Whatever associations about the term λόγος one could pull from Greek philosophical traditions are not terribly relevant." In fact, he adds that there is not a shred of evidence that John is even familiar with these Greek philosophies.[262] While Schenck sees some links, he qualifies them in the following way: while

---

[252] Hannah, *Michael and Christ*, 77.

[253] Dunn, *Christianity in the Making*, 221.

[254] Adam Kamesar, "The Logos Endiathetos and the Logos Prophorikos in Allegorical Interpretation: Philo and the D-Scholia to the Iliad," *Greek, Roman and Byzantine Studies* 44 (2004): 163.

[255] Tobin, "The Prologue of John and Hellenistic Jewish Speculation," *CBQ* 52 (1990): 256.

[256] Westcott, *The Gospel According to St. John,* xvii.

[257] Runia, "Philo of Alexandria," in *Routledge Encyclopedia of Philosophy*, 358.

[258] Nash, *The Gospel and the Greeks*, 72.

[259] Schenck, *A Brief Guide to Philo,* 89.

[260] Wolfson, *Philo*, 113.

[261] Harris, *Prologue and Gospel. The Theology of the Fourth Evangelist*, 197.

[262] Hurtado, *Lord Jesus Christ,* 366.

Philo's concepts are Platonic, John does not have any of these concepts.[263]

Third, there is no evidence that supports John's dependence on Philo. Herman Waetjen asserts that there is no evidence of direct dependency by John on the writings of Philo.[264] On the question concerning the direct influence of Philo on the background of John, Dunn asserts, "There is in fact no clear evidence favoring an affirmative answer."[265] Nash states that it is unnecessary.[266]

Fourth, Philo's writings suffer from inconsistency, contradictions, and lack of clarity. They are filled with misused quotations, confusing allegories, unclear concepts, and misuses of Greek grammar. Wolfson states that Philo did not treat philosophical problems systematically. [267] Runia states that Philo's concept of the λόγος is not "philosophically consistent." [268] Westcott describes the treatment of Philo's concept of the λόγος as sometimes personal, then impersonal, sometimes as an attribute, and sometimes as a second god.[269] Gerald Downing points out that even Philo acknowledges the limitation of his metaphors and choices of words, and that they

---

[263] Schenck, *A Brief Guide to Philo,* 89.
[264] Herman C. Waetjen, "Logos Pros Ton Theon and the Objectification of Truth in the Prologue of the Fourth Gospel," *Catholic Biblical Quarterly* 63 (2001): 266.
[265] Dunn, *Christianity in the Making,* 216.
[266] Nash, *The Gospel and the Greeks,* 77.
[267] Wolfson, *Philo,* 97.
[268] Runia, "Philo of Alexandria," in *Routledge Encyclopedia of Philosophy,* 359.
[269] Westcott, *The Gospel According to St. John,* xvii.

are not appropriate for the description of God. [270] Wolfson provides several insights about this: Philo utilizes allegorization "without any reservation."[271] Furthermore, he adds, "Everything in scripture, from names, dates, and numbers to the narration of historical events or the prescription of rules from human conduct, is to him subject to allegorical interpretation." [272] Moreover, "there is no attempt to adhere...to one consistent technical set of terms of one school."[273] This is a reason for this: It is the symptom of syncretism in which two diverse contradictory systems are placed together: OT and Platonism.

Fifth, the concept of the λόγος in John and Philo are strikingly different. While the λόγος is used in both writings, and while both writings heavily depend on the Old Testament, there is an unbridgeable gap. Carson recognizes the dualism that occurs in Philo's description of the λόγος and adds, "But Philo's λόγος has no distinct personality, and does not itself become incarnate. John's λόγος doctrine, by contrast, is not tied to such dualism."[274] Schnackenburg suggests that the difference is not just in the concept, but in the way they use the Old Testament:

> There is great gulf between the more typological use which John makes of the O.T., with the constant reference to Christ, and the allegorical and philosophical interpretation of Philo.[275]

---

[270] F.G. Downing, "Ontological Asymmetry in Philo and Christological Realism in Paul, Hebrews and John," in *Journal of Theological Studies* 41 (1990): 428.
[271] Wolfson, *Philo*, 116.
[272] Wolfson, *Philo*, 116.
[273] Wolfson, *Philo*, 97.
[274] Carson, *The Gospel According to John*, 115.
[275] Schnackenburg, *The Gospel According to St. John*,125.

Sixth, there are historical and literary problems that prohibit any dependency between John and Philo. Brown states that the philosophical coloring that is found in Philo is not found in John.[276]Brown adds, "We have no clear evidence that Philo's work was known in early 1st century Palestine."[277] Smalley adds that John never demonstrates literary dependence on Philo; nor is there any common ground, other than the Jewish background, that both share. He adds that their approach is different, one is historical and the other is philosophical, and that their interpretation is different, especially Philo's "insistent allegorizing." [278]

It is not surprising that the majority of scholars reject Philo's writings as a direct background for the λόγος of John. There are some links suggested; however, Masanobu Endo argues that when each link is examined carefully within its context:

> It becomes clear that these mediator figures were basically vivid ways of speaking of God's own power and activities (not as the hypostatic existence of these entities), or the way of solving theological and exegetical problems (in particular against the polytheistic views).[279]

Evaluation of Philo's System

The focus of evaluating the system of Philo should not be on the OT passages and entities Philo utilized, nor on his various

---

[276] Brown, *The Gospel According to John*, LVIII.
[277] Brown, *The Gospel According to John*, LVII.
[278] Smalley, *John Evangelist & Interpreter*, 64.
[279] Masanobu Endo, *Creation and Christology* (Tübingen: Mohr Siebeck, 2002), 5.

readings in the OT text to justify his system. The focus should be on the articulated λόγος concepts, for the goal is to retrieve the background of the concept. The following is the evaluation of Philo's system in accordance to the criteria of the Prologue of John:

1. John's λόγος is eternal without origin. Philo's λόγος is not eternal. It can be described as everlasting, but only in the context that it is indestructible. As Wolfson states, "Never does Philo describe the ideas as ungenerated."280

2. John's λόγος is the creator and was not created. Philo's λόγος is created before everything else and its contribution to creation is in the sense that it was the archetype of the world, as Wolfson also asserts.281 Schnackenburg articulates this point about John's λόγος:

He is not merely a way of speaking of the creative power of God or of the forms according to which God created the world. Since he is fully divine, he cannot be reduced to an intermediate stage; since he is a person, he cannot be dissolved into an idea.[282]

3. John's λόγος is a person while Philo's λόγος is impersonal.

---

[280] Wolfson, *Philo*, 209.
[281] Wolfson, *Philo*, 232.
[282] Schnackenburg, *The Gospel According to St. John,* 241.

4. John's λόγος is always with God in loving communion. Philo's λόγος is not.283 In fact, it has limited access to God.

5. John's λόγος has become flesh. Philo urges men to flee from the physical to attain the spiritual, and that the perfection of the divine λόγος is because it is not tainted by the physical world.

6. John's λόγος is God. In Philo's view, God does not partake of the λόγος.

The following are some of the differences in methodology:

1. Platonism is absent from John's Gospel. However, it dominates Philo's writings.

2. John's concept of λόγος stems from the theology of the OT, as the exegesis of the relevant OT texts demonstrates. On the other hand, Philo relies heavily on allegorizing of the OT to read in it his syncretistic system.

3. John is highly concerned with the prophetical aspect of the Old Testament. His focus is on who the Messiah is and how that Messiah is Jesus.[284] Philo is highly concerned with his impersonal syncretistic λόγος and to read it in the OT. His approach is philosophical at the expense of the prophetical aspect, thereby reducing the prophetical text to humanistic symbols of a philosophical concept.

---

[283] Wolfson, *Philo*, 201.
[284] Carson, *The Gospel According to John*, 663.

Dodd states that the striking difference between the Prologue and Philo are the philosophical methods of Philo, in which the λόγος is neither personal nor incarnate; the only personal attribute of it lies merely in "a fluctuating series of metaphors." [285]

Response to Modern Theories

Some scholars still support Philo as a background in certain contexts. They are divided into three categories:

First, some propose that Philo is a useful background that links wisdom literatures with the λόγος. One of the best arguments against the wisdom background is the lack of wisdom-specific terminology in the Prologue. Therefore, those scholars believe that the wisdom background provides the concept, and Philo provides the λόγος term. Tobin believes that Philo's writings constitute the connection between Wisdom and the λόγος; and furthermore, Philo's writings are the intermediate background between the wisdom literature and John's Prologue.[286] In particular, Tobin claims that the λόγος of Philo is the instrument through which the world was formed and that is the connection to the Prologue of John.[287] The problem with this view is the following:

1. The term λόγος in Philo is already associated with incompatible concepts with the λόγος of John.

---

[285] Dodd, *The interpretation of the Fourth Gospel*, 73.
[286] Tobin, "The Prologue of John and Hellenistic Jewish Speculation," in *CBQ* 52 (1990): 256.
[287] Tobin, "The Prologue of John and Hellenistic Jewish Speculation," in *CBQ* 52 (1990): 258.

Philo's concepts are associated with his own terms, and therefore, if Philo is to be used as any kind of bridge, then his concepts are unavoidable. Therefore, Philo cannot be an intermediate background between Wisdom and John.

2. There is no evidence for Philo acting as an intermediate background between John and any other system. The different concepts between John and Philo, especially in regards of the concept of the λόγος, suggest that John was not dependent on Philo.

3. Philo does not unite Wisdom and λόγος, but treats them as separate entities, and maintains the distinction in gender. In spite of this, Philo still assigns high honors to Wisdom. Why would Philo write a significant amount of material about Wisdom, treat her with honor, and maintain the distinction with Reason? The answer is that Philo's aim was to bring Platonic Reason into the Jewish faith, rather than replace Wisdom.

Second, there are scholars who propose that Philo provides the λόγος term and some simplified concepts. In other words, they acknowledge that the full concepts of Philo are not compatible with John, but they are satisfied with taking a simplified version of the concepts of Philo. Waetjen sees parallelism between John and Philo in that they both describe the λόγος as the agent of creation.[288] Runia also asserts the agent

---

[288] Waetjen, "Logos Pros Ton Theon and the Objectification of Truth in the Prologue of the Fourth Gospel" in *Catholic Biblical Quarterly* 63 (2001): 269.

of creation link.[289] Several opponents of this view have been mentioned before, such as Wolfson[290]. The following are the problems with this view:

1. The expression, 'the agent of creation,' is not helpful. It is a generic expression that masks deep problems. In Philo, the λόγος is the agent of creation, in that God created the λόγος as a model, and then God created the physical universe from the model. The model did not create the physical universe. In John, the λόγος is not created, but is the creator of everything. In other words, simplified or generic concepts do not solve the conceptual gap between the two systems.

2. Even if one takes a generic concept with generic terminology how is that better than the LXX description of the λόγος as the agent of creation without the influence of Greek philosophy.

3. The worldview of the λόγος in John is very different from the one in Philo. Furthermore, the nature of the λόγος is different.

The third category is represented by the work of James Dunn. Dunn starts the investigation with the Old Testament as the legitimate starting candidate background of the λόγος.[291] He examines only those verses that have the term λόγος and which offered personification.[292] He looks at very few specific verses,

---

[289] Runia, *Philo of Alexandria and the Timaeus of Plato*, 447.
[290] Wolfson, *Philo*, 285.
[291] Dunn, *Christology in the Making*, 216.
[292] Dunn, *Christology in the Making*, 218-219.

and he concludes that they are not the desired background.[293] Then he moves directly to Philo's writings, since they are the next writings that contain the λόγος, "which is entirely separate from the world we perceive by our senses and which can be known only by the mind."[294] Everything a human mind can know about the universe is through the model. Furthermore, the creator is known through his creation, namely the model. Dunn proposes the idea that everything that can be known about God is in this model, namely the λόγος. Therefore, the λόγος is the intermediary between God and man.[295] Elizabeth Harris describes Dunn's view as follows:

> Philo's logos is 'what is knowable of God; the logos is God in so far as he may be apprehended and experienced'. Significantly, he sees Philo's importance in the fact that his writings demonstrate 1) the sort of cosmological speculation widespread at the time of the evangelist, and 2) the fact that Jews could use such speculation without compromising their monotheism.[296]

Dunn applies his hypothesis onto the Prologue of John in the following manner: Dunn states that both the λόγος in Philo and in John are not personal, but impersonal. The λόγος of John became personal in the incarnation.[297] He then asserts that the λόγος is not the personal God but a manifestation of God. As one cannot know God fully but sees a smaller image of him in the λόγος of Philo, the same applies to the λόγος of John. He is

---

[293] Dunn, *Christology in the Making*, 220.
[294] Dunn, *Christology in the Making*, 221.
[295] Dunn, *Christology in the Making*, 226-227.
[296] Harris, *Prologue and Gospel. The Theology of the Fourth Evangelist*, 201.
[297] Dunn, *Christology in the Making*, 243.

not the personal God, but a smaller god that represents the manifestation of God. This is based on the usage of anarthrous θεός to describe the λόγος.[298]

There are several problems with this hypothesis:

1. Downing suggests that Dunn misrepresented the view of Philo in describing the λόγος as everything that is knowable about God, and that the λόγος is an intermediary being covering a gap between God and man.299 In fact, Wolfson asserts:

The conclusion we are forced to reach is that Philo had neither a logical nor historical reason to look for intermediaries, and if his Logos and powers and ideas are in some respects employed by God as intermediaries they are selected by Him for that task not because of the need to bridge some imaginary gulf between Him and the world.[300]

2. Dunn ignores the context of the Prologue of John. His view seems to suggest that, regardless of what is stated in the Prologue, the extrapolation of his hypothesis in Philo is a priori to the interpretation of the λόγος over the internal context. For example, Dunn suggests that the the λόγος is impersonal.[301] However, Murray Harris asserts, "everywhere in the Prologue the λόγος is portrayed as personal."[302]

---

[298] Dunn, *Christology in the Making*, 241.
[299] Downing, "Ontological Asymmetry in Philo and Christological Realism in Paul, Hebrews and John" in *Journal of Theological Studies* 41 (1990): 426-427.
[300] Wolfson, *Philo*, 289.
[301] Dunn, *Christology in the Making*, 243.
[302] Murray J. Harris, *Jesus as God: The New Testament Use of Theos in Reference to Jesus* (Grand Rapids: Baker, 1992) 59.

3. Dunn ignores the collective scholarship opinion on the exegesis of the λόγος. In particular, John 1:1c has already been extensively researched, and no credible scholar accepts that an anarthrous God means a lesser god; as David MacLeod asserts, "The divine λόγος fully shares in the Father's deity."[303] Carson responds to Dunn and asserts that Philo's argument is a deliberate maneuver to protect his monotheism, while in John, the omission of the article is "common Greek usage" based on a predicate nominative construction "which makes the alleged parallel in Philo irrelevant."[304]

4. Dunn ignores the historical context of the devotion to Jesus. Hurtado, in refutation of Dunn's view, states that Dunn underestimates the historical importance and evidence of early devotion to Christ as God.305

5. Dunn ignores the context of the Gospel of John. Murray Harris emphasizes that the context of the Gospel of John makes it clear that "the one whom John envisaged as preexisting with God" is "the pre-incarnate Son of God." 306 When reading the Prologue of John, there are clear parameters that are defined that cannot be overridden by any

---

[303] David J. MacLeod, "The Witness of John the Baptist to the Word: John 1:6–9" in *Bibliotheca Sacra* (2003), 73-74.

[304] Carson, *The Gospel According to John*, 137.

[305] Hurtado, *How on Earth did Jesus Become God*, 20.

[306] Harris, *Jesus as God*, 59.

background. These parameters determine the background and not vice versa.

The Term λόγος is from the OT

Wolfson offers an important insight concerning the background of the term λόγος that is used in Philo. He argues that Philo sought to interpret Scripture through Platonism, the result of which was that "The language of Scripture determines his choice of vocabulary in philosophy." [307] The various concepts he employs come from Greek philosophy, in particular Platonic philosophy; and his various terms come from Scripture. This is even truer for the usage of the term λόγος. Wolfson argues that Philo utilizes the concept of λόγος from Platonic philosophy, while he uses the term λόγος from the Old Testament.[308] Hannah states similarly that Philo's λόγος shows dependence on the Platonic concept of 'ideas.' Philo needed the λόγος to express the νοῦς of God, which was also portrayed in Aristotle.[309] Wolfson argues, convincingly, that the usage of the term λόγος by Philo was not because of the Stoics' vocabulary; otherwise, he would have followed their usage and their terms. [310] Moreover, Hannah states that the narrow range of λόγος in Greek philosophies does not support what Philo wanted to communicate. [311] In particular, Wolfson asserts that Philo needed a Scriptural term to communicate the concept of the Platonic νοῦς in terms of Scripture, since the term νοῦς was

---

[307] Wolfson, *Philo*, 97.
[308] Wolfson, *Philo*, 254.
[309] Hannah, *Michael and Christ*, 79.
[310] Wolfson, *Philo*, 253.
[311] Hannah, *Michael and Christ*, 80.

already reserved by Philo for the mind of man. The λόγος of the LXX provides various senses "as a means of the creation of the world, as a means of governing the world, and as a means of prophecy and revelation;" and so these various uses "helped to recommend itself to Philo as a substitute for the term νοῦς in the sense of the divine mind."[312] The same argument is made by Hannah as well. [313] This suggests that, at minimum, the background of the term λόγος comes from the OT.

---

[312] Wolfson, *Philo*, 254.
[313] Hannah, *Michael and Christ*, 80.

Wisdom

Wisdom Backgrounds

Evans states, "Johannine Christology is founded squarely on Old Testament language, imagery and concepts."[314] This book could have ended here after establishing that Philo's writings cannot be the primary background. However, the goal of this book is to establish that the Old Testament, without the later wisdom books, is the exclusive, primary background for the λόγος of John. There are three observations carried over from previous chapters that are instrumental:

First, it has been established that John is not limited by the LXX, and that in multiple occasions, he follows readings from the Hebrew Old Testament. This will be helpful when investigating Proverbs 8. In particular, the Hebrew text seems to provide a different meaning than the Greek text of the LXX.

Second, an important principle has been well articulated by Brown:[315] Whenever there are parallels or similar thoughts between two works, one should first investigate a common background shared by both. This common background is probably the relevant one for the system in question. This principle is as much true to Philo's writings as to Wisdom backgrounds. The question must always be asked, is there an ancestor background that contains the same ideas? If so, what

---

[314] Evans, *Word and Glory: On the Exegetical and Theological Background of John's Prologue*, 99.
[315] Brown, *The Gospel According to John*, LVIII.

prohibits the ancestor from being the true background for both systems? This will be relevant when investigating later wisdom literature.

Third, another principle is articulated by Westcott.[316]Utilizing the same terminology is not sufficient to establish a background. It is a question of doctrine and not terminologies. Therefore, when evaluating various backgrounds, one should ask the question about whether the background in question is one that explains the doctrines and concepts taught in the Prologue of John, or are the similarities superficial and merely utilizing similar terminology. This second principle is echoed by Carson:

> One reason why scholars are able to find parallels to John in so diverse an array of literature lies in John's vocabulary and pithy sayings. Words like light, darkness, life, death, spirit, word, love, believing, water, bread, clean, birth, children of God, can be found in almost any religion into which one probes.[317]

Dodd suggests that it is not merely Hebrew usage in the Old Testament, but also the theological concepts and elements of the Old Testament that support "the Logos-doctrine of the Prologue" which "can in great part at least be interpreted without much difficulty upon Old Testament presuppositions." [318] This principle will be essential in evaluating wisdom literature.

J. Rendel Harris is probably one of the first to suggest that Jewish wisdom literature is an important background for the

---

[316] Westcott, *The Gospel According to St. John*, XV.
[317] Carson, *The Gospel According to John*, 59.
[318] Dodd, *The interpretation of the Fourth Gospel*, 272.

λόγος of John.[319] Bultmann continues Harris' hypothesis, "The figure of Wisdom, which is found in Judaism, and also in the O.T. itself, does seem to be related to the Logos-figure in the Johannine Prologue."[320] Ben Witherington proposes that the wisdom of the Old Testament, for the most part, is the primary component of the Old Testament background that is fitting for the λόγος of John. He states that usage of the 'Word' in the OT does not provide enough personification, but that 'Wisdom' has the necessary elements to be a sufficient background for the Prologue hymn. In particular, he suggests:

> There one learns not just that personified Wisdom was present at creation, but also that she called God's people back to the right paths and offered them life and favor from God.[321]

While Proverbs 8 contains relevant material and should be included as part of the OT background, there are several considerations to be taken into account:

First, the general Wisdom background consists of primarily three literatures: Proverbs, the Wisdom of Solomon and the Wisdom of Jesus ben Sira. The latter two exhibit strong dependency on the Proverbs 8, as has been asserted by many scholars such as James Crenshaw[322] and Alexander Di Lella.[323] By combining Proverbs 8 with the general Wisdom background,

---

[319] J. Rendel Harris, *The Origin of the Prologue to St John's Gospel* (London: Cambridge University Press, 1917), 6.
[320] Bultmann, *The Gospel of John: A Commentary*, 22.
[321] Ben Witherington, *Jesus the Sage: The Pilgrimage of Wisdom* (Minneapolis: Fortress, 1994), 52.
[322] James L. Crenshaw, *Old Testament Wisdom: Introduction* (Louisville: Westminster John Knox Press, 2010), 217.
[323] Alexander A. Di Lella, *The Wisdom of Ben Sira* (New York: Doubleday, 1987), 332.

Proverbs 8 is considerably weakened. The reason for this is that the second-temple wisdom literature contradicts the parameters set forth earlier; especially when the later Jewish wisdom literature's worldview is allowed to dominate the interpretation of Proverbs 8. Therefore, Proverbs 8 is best seen as part of the Old Testament background in general, and not as part of the overall Wisdom background.

Second, the lack of wisdom terminology in the Prologue precludes any wisdom component or background from being the exclusive primary background, as Carson explains:

> The lack of Wisdom terminology in John's Gospel suggests that the parallels between Wisdom and John's Logos may stem less from direct dependence than from common dependence on Old Testament uses of 'word' and Torah from which both have borrowed.[324]

On the other hand, since Witherington suggests that the Wisdom component of the OT is the exclusive background, he provides the following reasoning for not using Wisdom in the Prologue:

> It may be that the evangelist simply used the term Logos to better prepare for the replacement motif- Jesus superseding Torah as God's Logos. Perhaps it was thought that the Logos concept better united creation and salvation history.[325]

Nevertheless, if wisdom is the exclusive background, there needs to be a link between Wisdom and λόγος. Philo's writings have already been excluded from being that link. Therefore, neither all Wisdom material in the OT is relevant, nor the

---

[324] Carson, *The Gospel According to John,* 116.
[325] Witherington, *Jesus the Sage,* 53.

relevant material, such as Proverbs 8, is the exclusive primary background. Instead, some of the verses of Proverbs 8 can be viewed as part of the OT background, especially when understood from the context of the rest of the Old Testament. Although Proverbs 8-9 are about wisdom in general, some selected verses in Proverbs 8 can be shown to be about the Son of God.

Proverbs 8

The relevance of Proverbs 8 for the λόγος of John hinges, for the most part, on the exegesis of one Hebrew verb in Pro 8:22, קָנָה (qănăh). There has been an extensive debate for the meaning of the verb קָנָה (qănăh) in the context of Proverbs 8. Some scholars understand it as 'acquire,' and others as 'create.' The proponents of the former understanding suggest that the meaning 'possess' is within the semantic domain of קָנָה (qănăh). If this is the case, then the text can suggest a divine creative entity with God. However, many Old Testament scholars object to the usage of Proverbs 8 as a reference about Christ. Michael Fox is one of the most important scholars to articulate that view. He states, concerning John 1:1-2, "The Logos was God from the beginning and apparently uncreated." [326] However, when it comes to the Wisdom of Proverbs 8:

> God acquired/created wisdom as the first of his deeds. Wisdom "was born" (vv 24, 25) at that time. She did not exist from eternity. Wisdom is therefore an accidental attribute of godhead, not an essential or inherent one.[327]

---

[326] Michael Fox, *Proverbs 1-9* (New York: Doubleday, 2000), 279.
[327] Fox, *Proverbs 1-9*, 279.

Despite the fact that Fox embodies the opposing view of this book, he is most helpful in the following: He articulates the main arguments of those scholars in his camp. He states:

> In my view, the question is moot. The word's lexical meaning, the semantic content it brings to context, is "acquire," no more than that. But one way something can be acquired is by creation. English "acquire" implies that the object was already in existence, but this is not the case with qanah. To avoid misunderstanding, the better translation in context is "created. While both "created" and "acquired" are legitimate contextual translations of this verb, "possessed" (Vul, KJV) is not. Though this mutes the theologically difficult implication that prior to creation God did not have wisdom, it does not really fit the context.[328]

Several points are made here:

1. The lexical meaning of קָנָה (qånåh) is 'acquire.'

2. A legitimate contextual meaning of קָנָה (qånåh) is 'create,' since something can be acquired through creation.

3. The semantic domain of קָנָה (qånåh) excludes the meaning 'possess.'

4. The context of קָנָה (qånåh) in Pro 8:22 requires the translation of 'create.'

5. Only the translation 'possess' solves the theological problem of God having no wisdom before its creation.

The following is the treatment of קָנָה (qånåh):

---

[328] Fox, *Proverbs 1-9*, 279.

First, the determination of whether Proverbs 8 can be used as a primary background for the λόγος of John hinges primarily on the exegesis of the Hebrew verb קָנָה (qānāh) in Pro 8:22. The LXX translates it as "created." Philo and wisdom literature follow the LXX. The other translation of it is strictly 'acquire/possess.' If the relationship between Yahweh and Wisdom is that of creation, then this is an unsuitable background for the λόγος of John. This is the second principle that Westcott and Carson spoke of earlier: It is not an issue of utilizing similar allegories or similar terminologies, but that of doctrine. This is important because most of proponents of the Wisdom background have no problem with Wisdom being created, but as Michael Fox articulated earlier, this does not fit. If the relationship between Yahweh and Wisdom is of creation, instead of eternal co-existence, as explained by Fox, then this is not a fitting background for the λόγος of John.

Second, All 83 (84 minus the instance in Pro 8:22) in the OT have been examined, these can be classified as following:

1. 62 references for 'purchase' or 'purchase with the intent of acquiring.' There is also the verb שׁבר (šbr) that means 'purchase of grain' and it occurs about 20 times. But this verb seems to be limited in that it does not give the sense of acquiring, so it cannot be utilized purchase a property, a land, or a slave. Therefore, קָנָה (qānāh) is the main OT Hebrew verb for 'purchase.' In many instances, it has been clearly contrasted with selling. Therefore, 'purchase' is a legitimate contextual meaning. Clearly, 'purchase' is not the intended meaning in Pro 8:22.

2. There are 15 instances with the meaning of 'acquire.' These are transactional instances in that the item acquired fits the idea that the owner did not have that item, a transaction occurred, then the owner acquired it. However, the focus is not the type of transaction, the focus that the item or entity was acquired. Clearly, this does not fit view of 'possess.' At the same time, this does not help the other camp because the focus is not on the transaction itself. In fact, the transaction is often not specified.

   a. One notable example is Gen 4:1 (KJV), I have gotten a man from the Lord. The transaction here is not clear: is it birth or is it a gift from Yahweh? If this is translated, as the ESV does, I have gotten a man with the help of the LORD, then the transaction is the help or the gift of the Lord. Then it is not correct to translate this as 'I gave birth to a man.' The verb here is not give birth. But the focus is not the transaction itself, it is the fact that she acquired a child, regardless of how she did.

3. There are 6 (7 minus Pro 8:22) instances that suggest the meaning of 'possess.' This is significant because if this is correct, then the claim of Fox is incorrect about the limitation of the semantic domain of קָנָה (qānāh) to the exclusion of 'possess.' Furthermore, the other Hebrew verbs that are used for 'possess,' such as יָרַשׁ (yāraš) and נָחַל (nāḥal),

Proverbs 8   *161*

suggest 'inheritance' or 'take possession of,' the exact semantic domain limitation that exclude the intended 'possess' meaning. In other words, קָנָה (qånåh) is possibly the appropriate verb to be utilized to donate 'possess,' for the other terms do not communicate the needed meaning. Furthermore, 'possess' would be a legitimate contextual meaning and translation if the context fits. In these instances, the focus is on ownership, personal knowledge, personal relationship, and love.

a. Isa 1:3, The ox knows its owner... But Israel does not know, my people do not understand. This verse contrasts the relationship between the ox and his owner, and between Israel and the Lord. The ox knows his owner. The focus here is not how the owner acquired the ox. A translation such as 'the ox knows his purchaser or acquirer' misses the point. The point is that the fact the ox knows him because he is the owner not because he purchased or acquired it.

b. Deut 32:6. The YLT renders it as follows, "Is not He thy father-thy possessor? He made thee and doth establish thee." There are three verbs associated with each other: קָנָה (qånåh), עָשָׂה ('åśåh), and כּוֹנֵן (kōnēn). The meaning of קָנָה (qånåh) here depends on the relationship between עָשָׂה ('åśåh) and

161

כּוֹנֵן (kōnēn). If these two are synonymous, then קָנָה (qånåh) can also be synonymous to them. However, they are not. The idea is that the Lord created them and then established [329] them. Then the better meaning of קָנָה (qånåh) is interpolated from the ordered set of the three verbs. I suggest that the proper meaning is 'Possess.' How would God possess Israel before they were created? The answer is through love. God loved Israel.

c. Gen 14:19 and 14:22 contain the following declaration, the owner of the heavens and earth. Translations are divided between 'owner/possessor of heaven and earth' and 'maker/creator of heaven and earth.' There are two perfectly serviceable Hebrew verbs for 'create,' עָשָׂה ('åśåh) and בָּרָא (bårå). These two words could have been used instead of the intended meaning is 'create.' Furthermore, the context suggests that in giving tithes, dividing spoil and enriching Abram, God is the owner of everything and He alone gets all the credit. This is suggested by the ESV rendering of Gen 14:22-23:

---

[329] HALOT suggests 'set up to last' and 'fix solidly.'

But Abram said to the king of Sodom, "I have lifted my hand to the LORD, God Most High, Possessor of heaven and earth that I would not take a thread or a sandal strap or anything that is yours, lest you should say, 'I have made Abram rich.'

d. Psa 139:13 (KJV), for thou hast possessed my reins: thou hast covered me in my mother's womb. This psalm contains a pattern:

  i. For thou hast possessed my reins. (deep knowledge of the Lord)

  ii. thou hast covered me in my mother's womb. I will praise thee; for I am fearfully and wonderfully made: Marvellous are they works; and that my soul knoweth right well. (creation)

  iii. My substance was not hid from thee (deep knowledge of the Lord

  iv. When I was made in secret, and curiously wrought in the lowest parts of the earth. (creation)

  v. Thine eyes did see my substance. (deep knowledge of the Lord)

  vi. And in the book all my members were written, which in continuance were fashioned, when as yet there was none of them. (creation)

The pattern emphasizes the deep knowledge of the Lord based on creation. So the first part is the deep knowledge, the second part is creation. Therefore, the best meaning for this instance of קָנָה (qånåh) is 'possess' with the implication of deep knowledge. The Lord possessed the internal parts: He had deepest knowledge in them: He owned them.

There are several conclusions here:

1. 'Possess' is a legitimate contextual meaning for קָנָה (qånåh) if the context allows it. In fact, it is possible the choicest verb to communicate this semantic flavor.

2. 'Create' is not a legitimate contextual meaning in any of the instance of קָנָה (qånåh) in the OT. In fact, it is impossible to present evidence for it according to R. N. Whybray.[330]

Third, some recently appealed to the rendering of קָנָה (qånåh) as 'beget.' Ugaritic text has been mind. Bruce Waltke provides a helpful summary:

> Of the nine occurrences of this root in Ugaritic having the possible meaning "create," as Cited by Gordon, once it means "obtain," once "create," two are uncertain, and five times it occurs in the epithet of Asherah as qnyt'lm, probably meaning "procreatress of the gods."[331]

---

[330] R. N. Whybray, *New Century Bible Commentary: Proverbs* (Grand Rapids: EERDMANS, 1994), 129.
[331] Bruce K. Waltke, *NICOT: The Book of Proverbs Chapters 1-15* (Eerdmans, 2004), 410.

There are several problems with this hypothesis:

1. If there is anything that can be concluded about the Ugaritic data is ambiguity. For they are divided among several meanings, the relevant 5 instances occur in non-verbal form in one epithet, there is insufficient data to determine if these are only a special term in epithet of Asherah, and there is no answer if this a semantic development from the idea of 'acquire, specific only to Ugaritic. There are more questions and neither sufficient nor convincing answers.

2. Why abandon 84 Hebrew instances for ambiguous 5 out of 9 Ugaritic instances? Appealing primarily to different language to determine the meaning of a term in another language is unreliable, although it is sometimes necessary as in the term אָמוֹן (ʾāmōn). However, in the case of קָנָה (qãnãh), it is unacceptable.

3. How come there is no single instance of קָנָה (qãnãh) in the OT that means beget? On the other hand, there is a serviceable consistent Hebrew word for beget, יָלַד (yãlaḏ). It is even used in Pro 23:22 (KJV), Hearken unto thy father that begat thee. Therefore, 'beget' is not a legitimate contextual meaning of קָנָה (qãnãh).

4. Fox argues repeatedly later that any meaning of birth or begetting falls under 'create.'[332] He is correct on this point. The idea of begetting in the

---

[332] Fox, *Proverbs 1-9*, 280-288.

OT implies that the entity did not exist before begetting. Therefore, the idea of 'create' is the intended meaning.

Fourth, Fox concedes the theological difficulty behind any rendering other than 'possess,' namely if God created wisdom, are we to assume that God was without wisdom before that special act of creation? [333] However, this is not a mere theological difficulty, it is at the heart of the exegesis of the book of Proverbs. Repeatedly in Proverbs, the call is for humans to acquire wisdom and knowledge. This occurs in Pro 1:5, 4:5, 4:7, 15:32, 16:16, 17:16, 18:15, 19:8, and 23:23. If humans are urged to acquire wisdom, are we to say that the Lord did not have wisdom but only acquired it later? If קָנָה (qānāh) is the Hebrew verb to express possession, in the correct context, then one would expect that it is used of the Lord. In other words, 'possess' is the default meaning here. It is the obligation of other camps to provide such overwhelming evidence to the contrary.

Fifth, when reading various commentaries, every camp insists that the context of pro 8:22-31 supports their reading. Nevertheless, an exegesis of this passage will demonstrate that the easy reading of it in context fits the 'possess' point of view.

A. Pro 8:22. There are several possible ways to translate 8:22. The first part is 'the Lord has possessed me'. The second part can be translated as 'as the beginning of his work,' 'in the beginning of his way.' דַּרְכּוֹ (darkō) in OT usage implies the works of God. The latter rendering is temporal and the former is a second direct object. Both are legitimate rendering of רֵאשִׁית דַּרְכּוֹ (rēšīt darkō). The temporal rendering is supported by the

---

[333] Fox, *Proverbs 1-9*, 279.

fact that קָנָה (qānāh) does not take a second object and hence the addition of 'as.' The second direct object is supported by the fact that the third part already communicates temporal sense. What is very attractive about the second direct object rendering is the parallel terms of the LXX and Rev 3:14: ἀρχὴν ὁδῶν αὐτου (archēn hodōn autou) versus ἡ ἀρχὴ τῆς κτίσεως τοῦ θεου (hē archē tēs ktiseōs tou theou), Christ is described as the beginning of the creation of God which is identical term here since the ways of God are his works. Third, רֵאשִׁית (rēšīṯ) could either mean first fruits or beginning. It cannot mean the first one to be created because he is described as eternal. Therefore, Wisdom is the beginning of creation. This is a theological title that requires definition. Graig Koester provides two possibilities in his commentary on Rev 3:14: Christ is either the Ruler of creation, or he is the origin/source of creation in that he is the divine creator.[334] The third part can be translated as 'before his creation of old' or 'before creation, from eternity'. Some take קֶדֶם (qeḏem) as 'first' but that is a stretch of the semantic range of the term. In checking all of the Hebrew instances in the OT, there are three possibilities: 'east,' 'Ancient/Eternal,' or 'before.' 'Before' makes more sense and fits the context best. מֵאָז (mē'āz) is best understood 'from old' which in absolute construction 'from eternity.' Therefore, Yahweh possessed Wisdom as the Creator of his works before creation from eternity. Wisdom was with Yahweh from eternity. There is a relationship between Wisdom and creation in that Wisdom was present during creation. If Wisdom was created, wisdom could not have been before creation. Is there a possibility that Wisdom was created before creation? This is probably not the case based

---

[334] Craig R. Koester, *The Anchor Yale Bible: Revelation* (Yale, 2014), 336.

on the following arguments: First, verse 23 states that Wisdom was eternal. Second, the emphasis of the third clause on 'before creation' suggests that eternity is the intended meaning. Third, if Wisdom existed only at a certain point, does this indicate that God was without Wisdom? Even if Wisdom is taken as an attribute of God, it has to be eternal. This is what John 1:1a states that in the beginning, the λόγος was already there. This is also consistent with Gen 1:1, in the Beginning God was already there before creation. Therefore, Wisdom was already there from Eternity; and from Eternity, Yahweh acquired Wisdom for special task which is to be the owner of creation and the architect.

B. Pro 8:23. Verse 23 provides an exact poetic parallel of Verse 22. It can be translated as "From eternity I was appointed before the beginning of the earth or before the earth was." ESV utilizes "set up" instead of "appointed". The Hebrew verb נָסַךְ (nāsāk) literally means "to pour". It is mostly used to indicate pouring of oil for dedication or anointing. When it is used on a person, Psa 2:6 provides a great example. ESV renders it as follows, "As for me, I have set my king on Zion, my holy hill." Whether it is installed, set up, or appointed, they all mean the same. There is a dedicated word for anointed in Hebrew, מָשַׁח (māšaḥ). However, this word can mean that the person or entity anointed is not present now but will be present later. נָסַךְ (nāsāk), on the other hand, requires that the person or entity to be present during set up or installation. From Eternity, the Wisdom has been appointed before creation. The Wisdom has been appointed for the Act of creation itself. Fox argues for the meaning of 'form' instead of 'appoint'.[335] HALOT suggests the meaning 'be

---

[335] Fox, *Proverbs 1-9*, 281.

woven or formed.'[336]   However, נֶסֶךְ (nāsāḵ) is never used to denote creation or formation of a non-physical entity. It was used to denote the pouring of liquids or the installation, or appointment of a King by pouring oil on him. Furthermore, HALOT suggests the meaning 'consecrated' or 'exalted' for Psa 2:6.[337] Ps 2:6 is closer to Pro 8:23. Verse 23 repeats the idea of verse 22. In order for Fox to argue against this position, he has to make an exceptional argument not just for קָנָה (qānāh) but also for נֶסֶךְ (nāsāḵ). Brown states that, Pro 8:22-23 supports the idea that Wisdom "existed with God from the beginning even before there was earth."[338] Barrett takes this thought further:

> A much more important line of approach is given by the Jewish concept of wisdom (Hokhma, Sofia). Already in Proverbs (see 8:22 quoted above) the wisdom of God has ceased to be merely the quality of being wise; wisdom has an independent existence in the presence of God, and also bears some relation to the created world. She remains also a blessed gift to man (8.24).[339]

C. Pro 8:24-25. Verses 24 and 25 state: before everything, I was brought forth. The Hebrew word for 'I was brought forth' is חוֹלָלְתִּי (ḥōlālətī). The form of this verb occurs only in three verses in the Old Testament. In addition to verses 24, and 25, it also occurs in Psa 51:7. The literal translation of it is "bring forth". Fox argues for 'born' and associates born with creation, instead of the association with bringing forth.[340] Nothing in the meaning of the word requires the understanding of creation

---

[336] *HALOT*, s.v., "נֶסֶךְ."
[337] *HALOT*, s.v., "נֶסֶךְ."
[338] Brown, *The Gospel According to John*, CXXIII.
[339] Barrett, *The Gospel According to St. John*, 153.
[340] Fox, *Proverbs 1-9*, 282.

(birth). Other words can be used to express the act of creation. It is another parallel to verses 22 and 23. In this case, Wisdom was brought forth or made to appear to assist in creation. But what does it mean to bring forth? This is a theological question first and foremost. From a Trinitarian perspective, this is not an ontological bringing forth, nor is it statement of origin. It is a functional manifestation of Wisdom for the special act of creation as the Artisan.

D. Pro 8:27-29. Verses 27-29 state from NKJV:

> When He prepared the heavens, I *was* there, When He drew a circle on the face of the deep, When He established the clouds above, When He strengthened the fountains of the deep, When He assigned to the sea its limit, So that the waters would not transgress His command, When He marked out the foundations of the earth.

The idea in this text is that during the planning for creation, Wisdom was there. This is consistent with verse 30 where Wisdom claims to be the creator. Initially, God planned all creation, and Wisdom was there and participated. Then Wisdom creatively implemented the plan of God. All of this happened before creation.

E. Pro 8:30. NLT states, "I was the architect at his side. I was his constant delight, rejoicing always in his presence." There are two elements in this text. The first element is that the Wisdom was the creator. The Hebrew word is אָמוֹן ('āmōn). It is 'artisan' in HALOT. Fox claims that it should be translated as infant or nursling because Wisdom cannot be an agent of creation.[341] Yet Whybray asserts that there is no evidence at all

---

[341] Fox, *Proverbs 1-9*, 286.

for the meaning of nursling.[342] Furthermore, Waltke claims that Fox's approach "is grammatically questionable."[343] Moreover, the context is clearly about creation. On the other hand, Waltke suggests that 'faithfully' "best suits the broader context" of the text,[344] which seems attractive when taken with Rev 3:14. Fox concedes that this is a very difficult passage to interpret.[345] The lack of other instances in the OT is a difficulty for whatever rendering is taken. But there are two helpful parameters: First, the idea of "nursling" is result of grammatical massaging that is not supported anywhere and therefore it can be safely eliminated. Second, the context of this text is that Wisdom is the creator who accompanied the Lord in his planning of creation. Therefore, the 'artisan' rendering is the most likely interpretation and is the most supported by scholars. This is consistent with John 1:3. The second element is that there was some fellowship between God and Wisdom. Wisdom was God's delight. Wisdom was happy in the presence of God. This is found also in John 1:1b. Bruce refers to this verse in relation to John 1:3 and he states that "all things exist by his Wisdom."[346] Furthermore, Bruce suggests a possible relationship between John 1:3, Pro 8:30, and Rev 3:14 in which "the 'Amen' maybe a variant of the Hebrew 'Amon', 'master workman', of Pro 8:30".[347] Carson makes the same suggestion.[348]

F. Pro 8:31. ESV states, "rejoicing in his inhabited world and delighting in the children of man." Wisdom is described as

---

[342] Whybray, *New Century Bible Commentary: Proverbs*, 136.
[343] Waltke, *NICOT: The Book of Proverbs Chapters 1-15*, 420.
[344] Waltke, *NICOT: The Book of Proverbs Chapters 1-15*, 421.
[345] Fox, *Proverbs 1-9*, 285.
[346] Bruce, *The Gospel & Epistles of John*, 32.
[347] Bruce, *The Gospel & Epistles of John*, 32.
[348] Carson, *The Gospel According to John*, 118.

having interest in humanity. Wisdom is portrayed in this verse as a mediator interested in interaction with humans. Humans are singled out of all creation. Wisdom is portrayed as a communicator with humans or as the λόγος of John. It might also suggest a pre-incarnation parallel to John 1:14. Brown supports this suggestion.[349]

G. Pro 8:35. ESV states, "For whoever finds me finds life and obtains favor from the LORD." This might be taken as a parallel to John 1:4, in that as the λόγος is the source of Life, so is the Wisdom the source of Life. Barrett suggests the relationship between John 1:4 and Pro 8:35.[350]

In summary, Pro 8:22-31 suggests that there is a divine person that is eternal, skilled, and was with God during creation. He was also in a personal joyful relationship with God. All of these attributes might suggest an important parallel to the Prologue. However, there needs to be more evidence that suggests that this is a distinct Person and not simply an attribute of God. Pro 30:4. ESV states:

> Who has ascended to heaven and come down? Who has gathered the wind in his fists? Who has wrapped up the waters in a garment? Who has established all the ends of the earth? What is his name, and what is his son's name? Surely you know.

A notable parallel exists between Pro 8:22-31 and Pro 30:4. Both passages mention acts of creation, design, and establishment of various elements. One passage mentions Wisdom as a companion of God. The other mentions the Son of

---

[349] Brown, *The Gospel According to John,* CXXIII.
[350] Barrett, *The Gospel According to St. John*, 157.

God. This parallel in the book of proverbs suggests that probably these two passages are related. If this is the case, then the Wisdom figure in Pro 8:22-31 is identified as the Son. This link is significant for John, since he alludes to Pro 30:4 in John 3:13.

Bruce states that verse 2 of the Prologue of John is not a repetition of verse 1, but an indirect reference to Pro 8:22-31. Therefore, when John 1:2 refers to the λόγος who was with God in the beginning, "[John] is probably referring to passages where divine wisdom is personified and described as being present and active at the creation of the world." [351] This, however, needs to be placed within several boundaries. First, there is the assertion of this book that Pro 8:22 does not describe a created entity but an uncreated entity that was always in existence with God. If this is not true, then Proverbs 8 becomes a secondary influence at best. What Michael Fox stated earlier is true about this. If it is created, then it is probably not a primary background for the Prologue of John. Second, even if Proverbs 8 is part of the OT primary background, it is not the exclusive component of the background. Proverbs 8 makes sense only in the context of the larger OT background.

---

[351] Bruce, *The Gospel & Epistles of John*, 31.

Ben Sira

Brown argues that the Wisdom in the later Jewish writings is the primary background, and it is closer to the Prologue of John than the Wisdom of the Old Testament.[352] He provides the most exhaustive parallel imagery between the Prologue and Wisdom Ben Sira. The proponents of this background, although they include the book of Proverbs in it, they maintain that the later Wisdom books are closer to the Prologue of John. They propose that these later literatures are an intermediate background between the wisdom of OT and the Prologue.

The following is a treatment of Wisdom ben Sira. Sir 1:1 states that Wisdom was with (μετά, meta) God, and will remain with him forever. Brown suggests a definite relationship to the Prologue of John on account of that Wisdom is portrayed as being with God. [353] Nevertheless, the justification for this background is that the later wisdom literatures are closer to the Prologue than the Wisdom of OT. However, Proverbs 8 already states that Wisdom was with God. It also states that Wisdom was in a relationship with God, mirroring the loving relationship with the Father in the Prologue of John. Wisdom ben Sira needs to provide either superior content or unique content that is not found in Proverbs 8. Any similarity found between Proverbs 8 and later wisdom literature suggests at best that Proverbs 8 is the

---

[352] Brown, *The Gospel According to John*, 523.
[353] Brown, *The Gospel According to John*, 522.

parent background of them and the Prologue. This similarity does not demonstrate dependency of John on the later wisdom literature. Definitely, it does not demonstrate, as Brown asserts, that later wisdom literature is superior to Proverbs 8 and OT in that regards.[354]

Moreover, that argument would have been relevant if Sira used πρός instead of μετά; for, John utilized πρός instead of μετά. Harris recognizes this problem to the extent that he appeals to Syriac in order to solve it.[355] However, the problem is not just the type of preposition used, but the idea behind the use of the preposition. According to the earlier exegesis of John 1:1b, πρός suggests, in the context of the Prologue of John, that the λόγος is a person, a concept greatly lacking in later second temple later literature.

Sir 1:1 states that "all wisdom" was with God. This is not the language to describe a person, but a property or virtue or an impersonal entity. This impersonal quality of Wisdom can be confirmed through the following: It is compared to prudence in Sir 1:4. Wisdom is compared to discipline in Sir 1:27. Sir 19:20 states that all of Wisdom is fear of God. Wisdom is also portrayed as human quality such as patience, prudence, and others, such as in Sir 1:23. Any personification of Wisdom is not more than any personification of other attributes of God, such as mercy and wrath, as seen as in Sir 5:6-7. Sir 1:8,10 states that God is the only wise one; he created Wisdom as a gift to humans. The gift of Wisdom can be attained by humans through following the commandments, according to Sir 1:26. Similarly, Sir 6:37 states that through the meditation on the

---

[354] Brown, *The Gospel According to John,* 523.
[355] Harris, *The Origin of the Prologue to St John's Gospel*, 7.

commandments of the Lord, he will grant insight and Wisdom. Sir 1:20 states that the root of Wisdom is the fear of the Lord. In other words, in order for humans to walk in Wisdom, they have to begin to fear the Lord. Wisdom is not any different from a property, a virtue, or an attribute of either God or godly humans. This is not different from the book of Proverbs' portrayal of Wisdom. However, Pro 8:22-31 is the exception. The language of that passage is highly personified to the extent that it is possible to interpret Wisdom as a person. The association with Pro 30:4 tips the scale towards personhood of Wisdom in Pro 8:22-31.

Furthermore, despite the fact that Sir 1:1 states that Wisdom was with God, it was not always with God, for it was created according to Sir 1:4, 1:8, and 24:9. Celia Deane-Drummond suggests that the portrayal of Wisdom as preexistent, especially in Pro 8 and Sir 24, provides John the language for his Prologue to articulate the same idea.[356] It is true that Pro 8 might provide such a link, but Sir 24:9 is unlikely since it states that Wisdom was created and not preexistent.

Sira praises Wisdom, but he also praises all other virtues and attributes of God, such as mercy and forgiveness in Sir 17:29. Sir 25:10-11 states that the fear of the Lord is greater than Wisdom. Furthermore, according to Sir 1:4, prudence was eternal while Wisdom was before all creation in the fact that it was created before creation. Roland Murphy suggests, "Wisdom

---

[356] Celia Dean-Drummond, *Christ and Evolution: Wonder and Wisdom* (Minneapolis: Fortress Press, 2009), 103.

is the peculiar quality of God that is manifest in creation because he lavished it upon his works."[357]

Sir 24:8 shows that Wisdom was ordered by God to pitch her tent among humans. Waetjin suggests that this is a link to the Prologue. [358] However, the meaning of this passage according to context is that Wisdom was given as a gift to the people of Israel, as seen in Sir 24:10-12. In fact, there is strong association between the Law of Moses and Wisdom, according to 24:23. Murphy suggests that Wisdom is the Torah. [359] Furthermore, Sir 14:25 urges men to pitch their tent near Wisdom. The expression of pitching a tent means to mentally perceive Wisdom and logically meditate on her, as also described in Sir 14:20-24. It is a downgrade from passages, such as Zech 2:10-11, in which the Lord, himself, pitched his tent.

Sir 4:27 states that whoever loves Wisdom loves life. Brown suggests some relationships between Wisdom and life.[360] However, Wisdom is not portrayed as source of life; instead, she is a guide to life. Moreover, how is this better than the material in the OT? Pro 3:18 states that Wisdom is a tree of life. In Proverbs 8, Wisdom calls all men and appeals to them because it has life to give. It is notable that the same passage, Sir 4:27, mentions those who seek her early in the morning. This is a reference to Proverbs 8.

---

[357] Roland E. Murphy, *The Tree of Life: An Exploration of Biblical Wisdom Literature* (Grand Rapids: Eerdmans, 1990), 135.

[358] Waetjen, "Logos Pros Ton Theon and the Objectification of Truth in the Prologue of the Fourth Gospel," *Catholic Biblical Quarterly* 63 (2001): 279.

[359] Murphy, *The Tree of Life: An Exploration of Biblical Wisdom Literature*, 139.

[360] Brown, *The Gospel According to John*, 522.

Bultmann states that the Wisdom suffered some rejection.[361] Probably, this is a reference to passages such as Sir 15:7. However, Isaiah 53 is a closer text of rejection.

Finally, there is no indication that Wisdom is an agent of creation. In fact, creation is solely attributed to God in many passages, such as Sir 16:26, 17:1, 24:8, and 43:33. Wisdom is neither eternal, nor creator, nor God, but it is a created impersonal entity.

---

[361] Bultmann, *The Gospel of John: A Commentary*, 22.

Wisdom of Solomon

Wisdom is portrayed as an impersonal attribute of God that comes only to righteous men as a kind spirit, according to Wis 1:5-7. In Wis 1:8, justice is also described in similar language as Wisdom. It is described as an agent of God that visits humans and administers punishments. Wisdom is equated to instruction in Wis 3:11. Wisdom is portrayed as an impersonal entity that ought to be learned as much as other holy things, according to Wis 6:9-11. Wis 7:7 shows that Wisdom is impersonal by equating her to 'understanding,' that was given by God to Solomon as a gift. Wis 7:16-17 and 8:21 repeat the similar ideas.

Wis 1:14 states that God created all things. There are many passages that attribute creation to God, such as Wis 2:23, 6:7, and 9:1. Yet, Wis 7:22 describes Wisdom as the craftsman of all things. Brown states that Wisdom is portrayed as an agent of creation.[362] David Winston suggests that this is derived from Pro 8:30, in which Wisdom is said to be the Architect.[363] John Collins states the same.[364] The context suggests the following meaning: Wis 7:16 states that all insight and knowledge of craftsmanship are in the hands of God, and Wis 7:17 states that God has given Solomon the knowledge of all that exists, and the

---

[362] Brown, *The Gospel According to John,* 522.
[363] David Winston, *The Wisdom of Solomon*(New York: Doubleday & Company, 1979), 176.
[364] John Collins, *Jewish Wisdom in the Hellenistic Age* (Louisville: Westminster John Knox Press, 1997), 197.

---

structure of the world. Therefore, Wisdom is the craftsman of all in that God has placed in Wisdom the knowledge of all things and how they are made. Furthermore, Wis 7:26 describes Wisdom as the mirror of God's work. In other words, Wisdom reflects to men the works of God. Finally, Wis 8:6 states that since understanding is effective, then it is worthy to be the craftsman of all. The context seems to suggest that Wisdom, or understanding, did not actively create anything. Instead, she is the craftsman of all because God placed the knowledge of creation in her; and therefore, since knowledge of how all things work is effective in making things, she is the craftsman of all. Thus, she reflects the work of God. There is probably an element of Platonism in these ideas in which Wisdom is equated to the world of forms or reflector of the world of forms.

The timing of when God placed that knowledge of creation in Wisdom is suggested by Wis 9:9. In particular, Wisdom knows of the works of God; it was present when God created the world. Winston suggests that this idea is derived from Pro 8:22.[365] Although there is no direct reference that states that God created Wisdom, it might seem that this would be the appropriate time for the creation of Wisdom. On the other hand, if Wisdom is an impersonal attribute of God, then it does not have to be created. But Pro 8:22 could not have been the only possible influence, for Wis 9:8 states that God made a copy of the Holy tent that was prepared beforehand. Here is a possible Platonic influence that speaks of forms prepared ahead of time in which Wisdom has the ability to reflect them to Solomon.

---

[365] Winston, *The Wisdom of Solomon*, 205.

Brown claims that in Wis 7:22, the adjective μονογενής (monogenēs) is applied to Wisdom in the sense of "unique.[366] However, the use of the term μονογενής is different from the way that the Prologue of John utilized it. In John, that term was utilized to express a unique loving relationship between the Father and the Son. The better background for the usage of μονογενής comes from Genesis from the relationship between Abraham and Isaac.

Waetjen claims that the λόγος of John is similar to Wisdom in "producing children of God."[367] This is a reference to Wis 7:27. However, the text is not about the new birth found in the Gospel of John. It is about Wisdom, an impersonal entity, making those who follow her moral precepts, closer to God.

Wis 7:25-27 is a curious passage that generated much speculation about Wisdom. Wis 7:25-26 glorifies Wisdom. Wisdom is described as a mirror and reflection of the power, the glory, and the goodness of God. Murphy sees Hellenistic influence in this.[368] Collins argues that this is emanation derived from Platonism although the author of the Wisdom of Solomon did not articulate a concrete philosophical system.[369] In order to address this passage, several questions need to be answered about it. Is Wisdom in this passage an attribute of God or is it a distinct entity? If it is a distinct entity, is it divine?

---

[366] Brown, *The Gospel According to John,* 522.
[367] Waetjen, "Logos Pros Ton Theon and the Objectification of Truth in the Prologue of the Fourth Gospel," *Catholic Biblical Quarterly* 63 (2001): 275.
[368] Murphy, *The Tree of Life: An Exploration of Biblical Wisdom Literature,* 143-144.
[369] Collins, *Jewish Wisdom in the Hellenistic Age,* 199-200.

First, Mcdonough suggests that Wis 7:27 portrays Wisdom as "a kind of force from God, or an emanation of God, a means by which he brings the world to its desired order."[370] Several scholars take the idea of emanation in this text to imply hypostasis - or a distinct entity in contrast to an attribute - to varying degree. Nevertheless, literary personification must not be discounted. The reason for this is that the context of the whole book suggests that Wisdom is nothing but an attribute of God. As have been stated earlier, the book of Wisdom describes Justice as visiting humans to administer punishments. Therefore, there is a pattern in describing the various attributes of God. This personification should not be quickly explained as hypostatic, given the context of the book. However, Collins identifies the language of this text with Platonic concepts, and therefore, he concludes, "Wisdom is an independent entity, which derives from God and reflects the divine glory, but then it becomes the means of God's presence in creation."[371] Mcdonough appeals to the context of the whole book; he responds, "This Wisdom is clearly God's Wisdom, rather than an independent being."[372] This might suggest that the author of the book of Wisdom took Platonic ideas and language and incorporated them in his Jewish worldview. This idea of the Wisdom emanating in the world is seen by Nash as an important Platonic influence on the book of Wisdom of Solomon.[373]

---

[370] Mcdonough, *Christ as Creator: Origins of a New Testament Doctrine*, 81.

[371] Collins, *Jewish Wisdom in the Hellenistic Age*, 199.

[372] Mcdonough, *Christ as Creator: Origins of a New Testament Doctrine*, 81.

[373] Nash, *The Gospel and the Greeks*, 72.

Second, is Wisdom divine in that passage? The goodness, power, and glory of God are reflected in his creation. As Wisdom helps humans understand the works of God, she reflects the goodness, power, and glory of God. Therefore, at best Wisdom is a tool created by God for that function. Based on the context of the whole book, Wisdom is probably not divine. Yet Winston states about this exact text, "This is very bold language indeed for someone who is writing within the biblical tradition."[374]

In summary, in Wisdom of Solomon, Wisdom is portrayed as an impersonal attribute or a virtue. Although, it was not explicitly mentioned that it was created, it was neither eternal nor God. One passage suggests that it is an agent of creation. However, the context suggests that it is only so in that it contained the knowledge of how things were created. Finally, Wis 7:25-27 might suggest that Wisdom is a divine hypostasis but it is not very conclusive.

There are three main arguments that support Wisdom of Solomon as a primary background for the Prologue.

First, many scholars, such as Brown[375], claim that Wisdom is an agent of creation. This is based on one verse, Wis 7:22. Murphy states that the role of Wisdom in creation is more explicit in Wisdom 7 than Proverbs 8, for he claims that the role of Wisdom in creation in Pro 8:30 is "ambiguous."[376] There are several problems with this.

---

[374] Winston, *The Wisdom of Solomon*, 184.
[375] Brown, *The Gospel According to John*, 522.
[376] Murphy, *The Tree of Life: An Exploration of Biblical Wisdom Literature*,144.

1. As has been stated earlier, Wis 7:22 is best understood as a reflector of what God has already created. This has been demonstrated earlier from the context of the book of Wisdom. This implies that the concept of agent of creation in the book of Wisdom is less evolved than Philo's ideas and not identical to it. At the least, Philo proposes that God created a model and used that model in creation. According to the book of Wisdom, Wisdom is an agent of creation in that it helps human see and appreciate what God has already created. There are some common themes between Philo's concept of agent of creation and the concept found in the book of Wisdom. Wolfson suggests that Wisdom is not an intermediary to God nor is an agent of creation; it did not create the world after it was created by God.[377] At the least, Wis 7:22 does not carry the same sense that is in the Prologue of John. The gap between the two concepts is huge. Schnackenburg articulates the intent of the Prologue:

> He is not merely a way of speaking of the creative power of God or of the forms according to which God created the world. Since he is fully divine, he cannot be reduced to an intermediate stage; since he is a person, he cannot be dissolved into an idea.[378]

2. It seems that the author of the book of Wisdom took the concept found in Proverbs 8 and Pro 3:19 and attempted to provide an explanation to them without violating his Jewish monotheism. At the same time, he utilized some Platonism for that. Pro 3:19 explicitly states that the Lord utilized Wisdom to create earth. The book of Wisdom made Wisdom the agent of creation in the sense of helping humans to understand the works

---

[377] Wolfson, *Philo*, 287.
[378] Schnackenburg, *The Gospel According to St. John*, 241.

of God. Mcdonough observes that the concept comes from the mind of a committed Jewish author.[379] Even Murphy maintains that that the author, despite Hellenistic influences, was "intensely Jewish."[380] However, the author's attempt to explain away Proverbs 8 diluted the original concept of Proverbs 8 and the rest of the Old Testament and pushed it into syncretistic worldview. The question is not how explicit the declaration of agent of creation is. The question is what the concept behind the declaration of the agent of creation is. In the regard of the concept of agent of creation, the declaration in Proverbs 8 is closer to the Prologue of John. Pro 8:30 states that Wisdom is a skilled artisan and the beginning of Yahweh's works. The context of Proverbs 8 suggests that God brought forth and utilized Wisdom as a skilled artisan to create. This is a closer parallel to John 1:3 rather than the idea that God created Wisdom and placed in her the knowledge of creation - or the idea of an attribute of God acting as a mirror reflecting previously made copies - to help humans understand the works of God.

Second, some scholars see Wis 7:22-27 as evidence for the divinity of Wisdom. Murphy states, "Her divine character is articulated in a manner that goes beyond the traditional 'begetting' in Pro 8:22-25."[381] Combined with that, Crenshaw sees Wisdom as 'hypostasis' in that passage, in that Wisdom is described as "pure emanation of the Creator."[382] He concludes, "This elevated concept easily prepared the way for the later

---

[379] Mcdonough, *Christ as Creator: Origins of a New Testament Doctrine*, 81.
[380] Murphy, *The Tree of Life: An Exploration of Biblical Wisdom Literature*, 174.
[381] Murphy, *The Tree of Life: An Exploration of Biblical Wisdom Literature*, 144.
[382] Crenshaw, *Old Testament Wisdom: Introduction*, 217.

Christian understanding of Jesus as the wisdom and word of God."[383] There are several problems with this view:

1. As has been shown earlier, it doubtful that Wisdom in that passage is an independent entity of God that is also deity. At one extreme, it is a personified impersonal attribute or property of God. At another extreme, it is an independent created tool, similar to the model of Philo. There is the possibility that it can be considered an independent deity, but then this by itself takes her outside of the doctrines of the OT and the NT. The Prologue of John is not about the emanation of a secondary deity, impersonal mirror, or an attribute of God. It is about God himself becoming flesh.

2. The concepts derived from this text are best compared to the concept of λόγος in Philo, for both exhibit Platonic influence. Winston suggests many significant parallels between the writings of Philo and this text.[384] Yet it has been shown that the λόγος of Philo is fully incompatible with the λόγος of John.

3. Proverbs 8 is closer to the Prologue of John than Wis 7:22-27. The reason for this is Proverbs 8 provides language that is more consistent with the concepts found in the Prologue. In order for this passage to be relevant to the Prologue of John, it must provide superior content. Proverbs 8 allows a distinct personal entity to be the creator beyond the literary personification. Murphy suggests that Wisdom of Proverbs 8 is more than mere personification, but the identification with and the revelation of God himself.[385] Moreover, when other verses

---

[383] Crenshaw, *Old Testament Wisdom: Introduction*, 217.
[384] Winston, *The Wisdom of Solomon*, 185-189.
[385] Murphy, The Tree of Life: An Exploration of Biblical Wisdom Literature,138.

of the OT are combined with Proverbs 8, such as Proverbs 30, the context of OT suggests that there is a second person within the one God.

Third, as stated earlier, many scholars suggest that there is similar language between later Wisdom literature and the Prologue. They also suggest that this similar language provides a link between the two. For example, Brown suggests that the application of the adjective μονογενής to Wisdom provides the link to the Prologue.[386] Evans suggests other parallels.[387] The most significant parallels were discussed earlier. There are several problems with this.

1. One of the most recognized obstacles for wisdom literature is the lack of explicit and distinctive wisdom terminology that ties them back together:

> The lack of Wisdom terminology in John's Gospel suggests that the parallels between Wisdom and John's Logos may stem less from direct dependence than from common dependence on Old Testament uses of 'word' and Torah from which both have borrowed. [388]

Although Nicola Denzey affirms that an important obstacle is the lack of wisdom terminology in the Prologue of John, he nevertheless suggests that scholars have found in Philo's writings a solution for that problem.[389] However, it has already

---

386 Brown, The Gospel According to John, 522.
387 Evans, Word and Glory: On the Exegetical and Theological Background of John's Prologue, 93.
388 Carson, The Gospel According to John, 116.
389 Nicola Denzey, "Genesis Traditions in Conflict? The Use of Some Exegetical Traditions in the Trimorphic Protennoia and the Johannine Prologue," Vigiliae Christianae 55 no 1 (2001): 27-28.

been demonstrated that this is not the case. [390] Furthermore, Denzey states that Johannine Prologue is not an example of wisdom literature. [391] However, terminology is not the only problem; the concept of Wisdom in later literature is incompatible with the Prologue of John.

2. All of these parallels or similar language are already found in the OT, and most of them are already found in the book of Proverb. In fact, most of them are found in Proverbs 8. In virtually all of them, the OT provides superior and deeper concepts that are closer to the Prologue of John. Furthermore, most of them are found in Philo's writings on the λόγος, and yet Philo does not meet the criteria for being a primary background. This is very consistent with the second principle: Terminology and imagery are not enough. It is all about doctrine.

3. Although later wisdom books borrowed from Proverbs 8, these books did not preserve the personification and concepts found in Proverbs 8. Instead, they developed Wisdom into an impersonal created entity. Schnackenburg states, "The personal character of the Logos forms a definite contrast to the Wisdom speculation of Hellenistic Judaism." [392] Furthermore, both the concept of λόγος in Philo and the concept of Wisdom in wisdom literature are downgraded to an impersonal entity. On the other

---

390 Denzey also suggests that the work of Jack T. Sanders on Odes of Solomon can also be a solution. Odes of Solomon do not contain a personified Logos, nor can they bridge between Wisdom and Logos. Furthermore, they are later work, not suitable to be the background of the Prologue.

391 Denzey, "Genesis Traditions in Conflict? The Use of Some Exegetical Traditions in the Trimorphic Protennoia and the Johannine Prologue," *Vigiliae Christianae* 55 no 1 (2001): 28.

392 Schnackenburg, *The Gospel According to St. John*, 233.

hand, Proverbs 8 allows Wisdom to be interpreted as person instead of the personification of an impersonal entity.

In conclusion, when it comes to the five elements of the Prologue of John, namely eternity, creator, deity, personhood, and incarnation, it is noteworthy that the Wisdom of Solomon fails. Wisdom is an impersonal, created entity. It was never described as God or eternal. Hurtado states, "The stark statement in John 1:1, "the Word was God," takes us noticeably beyond Wisdom tradition."[393] In fact, Hurtado reiterates that the background of the Prologue of John and the rest of the Gospel of John "is much more explicitly linked with God's name than with wisdom."[394] Based on the wisdom literatures, Mcdonough does not support equating Wisdom with the Messiah directly or indirectly.[395] Elizabeth Harris states the following about the Wisdom background:

> It does, however, as Dodd observes, still fall a good way short of the statement in the prologue that "the Word was God', and the visits of Wisdom to human beings, successful or unsuccessful, and her presence with them, do not have the same force as the incarnation at a single moment as veritably human of a divine pre-existent 'person'.[396]

What is seen as common imagery between the Prologue of John and second-temple wisdom literature is better explained by their dependence on a common ancestor background, namely, the OT.

---

[393] Hurtado, *Lord Jesus Christ*, 367.
[394] Hurtado, *Lord Jesus Christ*, 366.
[395] Mcdonough, *Christ as Creator: Origins of a New Testament Doctrine*, 83.
[396] Harris, *Prologue and Gospel. The Theology of the Fourth Evangelist*, 198.

Logos

Memra (מֵימְרָא)

Memra (מֵימְרָא, mēmərā̊) comes from the Aramaic Targums and its significance is that it is often used as circumlocution to the Tetragrammaton, as John Ronning puts it. [397] The importance of Memra is that it means 'word' in Aramaic. The reason it can be an attractive background because it suggests that John's intention from the λόγος is to refer to the personal name of God, namely YHWH. No doubt John spoke Aramaic, and in his gospel he refers to several Aramaic words. He possibly knew the word Memra and its usage. When John wrote about the λόγος, did he have Memra in mind? Brown suggest so; he offers examples in which the Memra replaces God in the Aramaic Targums to demonstrate the power of Memra:

> If in Exod iii 12 God says, "I will be with you," in the Targum Onkelos God says, "My Memra will be your support." If in Exod xix 17 we are told that Moses brought the people out of the camp to meet God, in Targum Onkelos we are told that they were brought to the Memra of God. If Gen xxviii 21 says, "Yahweh shall be my God," Targum Onkelos speaks of the Memra of Yahweh. [398]

[397] John L. Ronning, *The Jewish Targums and John's Logos* Theology, (Peabody: Hendrickson Publishers, 2009) 13.
398 Brown, *The Gospel According to John*, 524.

Ronning adds the following assertion: in examining the Targums from the context of Memra, "Memra conveys the being and doing of YHWH across the entire spectrum;" moreover, In the Targum, there is strong association between the name of God and the word of God. In fact, there are instances that they are used interchangeably. [399] There are several observations concerning this:

First, both Brown and especially Ronning in previous quotations implied that Memra's significance was not just for the name of God but also the association of the name, the works of YHWH with the word. Nevertheless, one does not need Memra to make such associations. In fact, in examining Ronning's hypothesis, he seems inadvertently to be arguing for the OT as the background.

Second, in the hypothetical case of accepting Ronning's view, Memra needs to be restricted to the background of the term not the background of the concept. The concept of λόγος encompasses wide and rich material from the Old Testament. What is attractive about the term λόγος is its wide semantic range that allows it to be relevant to all parallels of the OT.

Third, from theological perspective, Memra as a replacement for YHWH is an attractive proposition. It fits in the prologue. Yes, the λόγος is YHWH. But why Memra was not used instead of λόγος? And if the Greek language is the response, could John not provide translation for it as he has done repeatedly in his Gospel?

---

399 Ronning, *The Jewish Targums and John's Logos Theology*, 14.

Fourth, Barrett objects that Memra is not "truly hypostasis" but it is rather "speaking about God without using his name."[400] Keener also objects that Memra is not depicted as personal.[401] But one can respond that the intention is not Memra but the Tetragrammaton. This would work only if Memra is the background of the term and not the concept. Otherwise, the above objections are valid.

Fifth, the more astute problem is the lack of positive evidence that connects Memra with λόγος as a term that refers to YHWH. One might point out that the Gospel of John claims that Jesus is YHWH. While this is true, that is only one of the claims of the Gospel about Jesus; therefore, that fact cannot be used as the needed evidence. The λόγος seems to be a wider term encompassing the whole theology of the OT about the Son. In any case, Memra cannot be used as the primary background.

---

[400] Barrett, *The Gospel According to St. John*, 153.
[401] Keener, *The Gospel of John*, 350.

Background of the Term

If the Old Testament contains the concepts needed for the primary background, then what about the term λόγος? Does the Old Testament provide background of the term itself? The following are various thoughts and observations concerning the OT. Dodd proposes that the Hebrew language offers the needed personification of the Hebrew term 'word' to support such connection between it and the concept of the λόγος in John. In particular, he suggests that the Hebrew 'word' has its own substantive existence when it is spoken; and this is significant even if it can be explained away as some poetical function of the language:

> It must be nevertheless admitted that the readiness to use such language points to a habitual tendency of thought to attribute to the spoken word an existence and activity of its own; and in fact such a tendency is deeply impressed upon the Hebrew language.[402]

Brown provides the example of Isa 55:11 in which the word of God "exercises independent functions which are almost personal." What makes this verse more significant is the fact that Isaiah 55 forms the background for John chapter 6.[403] John's direct quotation from the passage in Isaiah, which contains a

---

[402] Dodd, *The interpretation of the Fourth Gospel*, 264.
[403] Brown, *The Gospel According to John*, 521.

reference to the word of God exhibiting some form of independent existence, is significant. For if John has referred to this passage, in all probability, the verse about the Word of God was on his mind. Keener asserts, "While OT Depictions of the Word by themselves probably do not constitute an adequate explanation of the Johannine prologue, OT personifications of the Word or expressions of its activity in creation are significant."[404]

Brown associates life with the word, "For the Deuteronomist the word is a life-giving factor (Deut 32:46-47)"[405] He also associates the word with light, "the word of God was also described in the OT as a light for men (Pss cxix 105,130, xix 8)"[406] Moreover, he associates creative functions with the word:

> The "word of the Lord" also had a creative function in the OT even as has the Word of the Prologue. We saw that the Prologue imitates Gen I, and there creation takes place when God says, "let there be light...." According to Ps xxxiii 6, "By the word of the Lord the heavens were established".[407]

Carson asserts that since John very frequently quotes or alludes to the Old Testament, this should be the starting point to look for an appropriate background. He then suggests many examples concerning the Hebrew word, דָּבָר, and how it is used in various passages of the OT in which it is used in creation (Gen 1:3, Psa 33:6), revelation (Jer 1:4; Isa 9:8; Ezek. 33:7; Amos 3:1,8), and deliverance (Psa 107:20; Isa 55:11). He explains:

---

[404] Keener, *The Gospel of John*, 351.
[405] Brown, *The Gospel According to John,* 521.
[406] Brown, *The Gospel According to John,* 521.
[407] Brown, *The Gospel According to John,* 521.

If the Lord is said to speak to the prophet Isaiah (e.g. Is. 7:3), elsewhere we read that 'the word of the Lord came to Isaiah' (Is. 38:4; cf. Je. 1:4; Ezk 1:6). It was by 'the word of the Lord' that the heavens were made (Ps. 33:6): in Gn. 1:3, 6, 9, etc. God simply speaks, and his powerful word creates. That same word effects deliverance and judgment (Is. 55:11; cf. Ps. 29:3ff.).[408]

F.F. Bruce also highlights the accounts of Genesis and the word of God:

The true background to John's thought and language is found not in Greek philosophy but in Hebrew revelation. The 'word of God" in the Old Testament denotes God in action, especially in creation, revelation and deliverance. In the creation narrative at the beginning of Genesis we read repeatedly that 'God said... and it was so'.[409]

Barrett makes an assertion that John's introduction to the term indicates that his readers are familiar with it. [410] The Old Testament is the background of the term λόγος.

---

[408] Carson, *The Gospel According to John,* 115.
[409] Bruce, *The Gospel & Epistles of John,* 29.
[410] Barrett, *The Gospel According to St. John,* 152.

The Primary Background

There are ample of parallels for the λόγος of the prologue of John. Carson states:

> One reason why scholars are able to find parallels to John in so diverse an array of literature lies in John's vocabulary and pithy sayings. Word like light, darkness, life, death, spirit, word, love, believing, water, bread, clean, birth, children of God, can be found in almost any religion into which one probes.[411]

However, the pursuit of a primary background is concerned with finding a parallel that explains the concepts. This primary background forms a dependency relationship with the Prologue of John. In other words, the Prologue John demonstrates conceptual dependence on the primary backgrounds. It is possible that a particular text has more than one primary background. For example, Philo's writings exhibit dependence on both OT and Platonic philosophy. The book of Wisdom of Solomon exhibits similar dependency. Furthermore, there are varying degrees of dependency. For example, Philo's dependence on Platonic philosophy is more concrete than that of the Wisdom of Solomon.

Finally, there is a direction of the dependency, which is the hermeneutical framework. For example, Philo searches various

---

[411] Carson, *The Gospel According to John,* 59.

OT passages to support his platonic ideas. He views and interprets the OT from such a hermeneutical lens. Wisdom of Solomon does something similar with their Wisdom entity. In contrast, John takes the concepts of the OT about God the Son to show that the Messiah taught in the OT is Jesus. As Carson states:

> The fundamental question being addressed by the Evangelist is not 'Who is Jesus?', which might be asked by either Christians or non-Christians, if with slightly different emphases; but 'Who is the Messiah?'.[412]

And as he states also:

> The fundamentally Jewish and Old Testament background to John's Gospel is increasingly recognized. What we call the Old Testament is what he repeatedly quotes, and that to which he repeatedly and explicitly alludes.[413]

One question remains: what is behind the choice of John for the term λόγος? The OT describes a λόγος entity that speaks on behalf of God to the prophets. It is given by God to perform his tasks. It is responsible for creation. It is associated with God. In the book of Proverbs, it is Wisdom. Wisdom is eternal and enjoys relationship with God. Wisdom was with God during creation and was a skilled artisan. In Proverbs 30 and in various texts of the OT, he is the Son who was with God during creation. In the book of Genesis, it is significant that speaking and creating are the first reported actions of God. In this case, John presents to us God the Son as the agent of revelation, agent of creation, and the beloved, unique one of the Father.

---

[412] Carson, *The Gospel According to John,* 663.
[413] Carson, *The Gospel According to John,* 59.

The OT does not just provide the concepts but also the terminologies. For example, the conceptual and linguistic parallel that is found in Proverbs 8 is one example. John 1:1a speaks of the eternity of the λόγος in that he was from the beginning. Pro 8:23 speaks of the eternity of Wisdom in that it was from the beginning. It is significant that it utilizes the same word 'beginning' to indicate eternity. John 1:1b speaks about the relationship between the λόγος and God in that he was with God. Pro 8:22, 27-30 speaks of the relationship between Wisdom and God in that Wisdom was with God from eternity. Wisdom was in an eternal, personal, and joyful relationship with God. John 1:1c states that the λόγος was God. Pro 8:24-29 is paralleled with Pro 30:4. Proverbs identifies Wisdom as the Son. Both Wisdom and the Son were the one entity that was with God during the design of creation. John alludes to Pro 30:4 in John 3:13 to identify the Son. If the λόγος is God in John 1:1c, then Wisdom is the eternal Son in Proverbs 8 and 30. John 1:3 states that the λόγος is the creator. Pro 8:30 states that the Wisdom is a skilled artisan. If Pro 8:22-31 can be viewed as a Hebrew poem, then conceptually, the Prologue of John can be seen as the Greek parallel to it.

The Son who is the Messiah in Proverbs 30, Isaiah 53, Isaiah 9, Isaiah 7, Isaiah 48, Micah 5, and other passages form another conceptual parallel. In addition to the association of Wisdom with the Son, these passages provide an important parallel to the Prologue. Proverbs 30 associates the Son with creation. Isaiah 53 associates the Son with rejection. Isaiah 9 states that the Son is God. Isaiah 7 and Isaiah 9 speak of the incarnation of the Son. Isaiah 48 speaks about the relationship of the Son with God. Micah 5 states the Messiah is eternal. It is notable that John quotes from Isaiah 53 in his Gospel.

The personified λόγος of the OT is connected to Wisdom of Proverbs. For in Psa 33:6, the λόγος is portrayed as the agent of creation. Isa 55:11 explains what is meant by the λόγος being the agent of creation: The λόγος is sent by God and is given to perform the works of God. The λόγος succeeded in fulfilling God's work. It is a proactive work of creation as much as Wisdom is portrayed as the skilled artisan. Creation is not the only task of the λόγος; God sends the λόγος to heal and to save in Psa 107:20. Furthermore, the personified λόγος is said to speak directly to the prophets in Jer 1:4. This is probably one of the strongest personifications of the λόγος in the OT. If the λόγος is portrayed as the agent of revelation and communication in the OT, the λόγος, the unique beloved of the Father, is said to be the agent of revelation and communication in John 1:18.

God the Son being the agent of revelation and communication is probably the reason why John chose the term λόγος. The conclusion of the Prologue, John 1:18, suggests that the Son was the one that communicated with the prophets of the OT. He is the λόγος that appeared to the prophets, spoke to them, visited with them, and performed the actions of God. Since the Old Testament is the overarching background, then Keener's insight is helpful, "It is more likely that John prefers Logos because "Word" had broader OT connotations." [414] This is significant for the term λόγος can probably be taken as generic enough to include all of the above parallels.

These are not the only significant parallels of the OT. The parallel that is found in the Angel of the Lord is important as well. The former parallels are offered to show the dependency of the λόγος of the Prologue on the OT material.

---

[414] Keener, *The Gospel of John*, 354.

This book proposes that the Old Testament is the exclusive primary background for the Prologue of John. This includes the Old Testament and all its components. The λόγος of the Prologue of John is the Son of God revealed in the Old Testament and in the Gospel of John (John 21:25).

Bibliography

Barrett, C.K. *The Gospel According to St. John: An Introduction with Commentary and Notes on the Greek Text*. Philadelphia: The Westminster Press, 1978.
—————. *The New Testament Background*. Harper Collins, 1987.

Bauer, W. *A Greek-English Lexicon of the New Testament and Other Early Christian Literature*. Rev. F. W. Danker. 3rd ed. The University of Chicago Press, 2000.

Borchert, Gerald. *An Exegetical and Theological Exposition of Holy Scripture*. Broadman & Holman Publishers, 1996.

Brown, F. Driver, S. Briggs, C. *The Brown-Driver-Briggs Hebrew and English Lexicon*. MA: Hendrickson, 2001.

Brown, Raymond E. *The Gospel According to John: Introduction, Translation, and Notes*. Garden City: Doubleday, 1966.

Bruce, F.F. *The Gospel & Epistles of John*. Grand Rapids: Eerdmans, 1983.

Bultmann, Rudolf. *The Gospel of John: A Commentary*. The Westminster Press, 1971.

Calvin, John. *John*. Wheaton: Crossway Books, 1994.

Carson, D. A. *The Gospel According to John*. Grand Rapids:
    Eerdmans, 1991.
————. *Exegetical Fallacies*. Grand Rapids: Grand
    Rapids: Baker Books, 1996.
————. "John 5:26: Cruz Interpretum for Eternal
    Generation." In *Retrieving Eternal Generation*. Edited
    by Fred Sanders and Scott R. Swain, 79-97. Zondervan,
    2017.

Collins, John. *Jewish Wisdom in the Hellenistic Age*.
    Louisville: Westminster John Knox Press, 1997.

Crenshaw, James L. *Old Testament Wisdom: Introduction*.
    Louisville: Westminster John Knox Press, 2010.

Dean-Drummond, Celia. *Christ and Evolution: Wonder and
    Wisdom*. Minneapolis: Fortress Press, 2009.

Denzey, Nicola. "Genesis Traditions in Conflict? The Use of
    Some Exegetical Traditions in the Trimorphic
    Protennoia and the Johannine Prologue." *Vigiliae
    Christianae* 55 no 1 (2001): 20- 44.

Di Lella, Alexander A. *The Wisdom of Ben Sira*. New York:
    Doubleday, 1987.

Dodd, C.H. *The Interpretation of the Fourth Gospel*.
    Cambridge: Cambridge University Press, 1954.

Downing, F.G. "Ontological Asymmetry in Philo and
    Christological Realism in Paul, Hebrews and John." In
    Journal of Theological Studies 41 (1990): 423-40.

Dunn, James D.G. *Christology in the Making: A New
    Testament Inquiry into the Origins of the Doctrine of
    Incarnation*. Philadelphia: Westminster Press, 1980.

——————————. "Let John be John – a Gospel for Its Time." In *Das Evangelium und die Evangelien*, edited by P. Stuhlmacher, 309-339. Tübingen: Mohr Siebeck, 1983.

Elliot, Mark. *Ancient Christian Commentary: Isaiah 40-66*. Intervarsity Press, 2007.

Endo, Masanobu. *Creation and Christology*. Tübingen: Mohr Siebeck, 2002.

Erickson, Millard J. *Christian Theology*. Grand Rapids: Baker Books, 1998.

Evans, Craig A. *Word and Glory: On the Exegetical and Theological Background of John's Prologue*. Sheffield Academic Press, 1993.

Evans, Craig A. Porter, Stanley E. *Dictionary of New Testament Background*. Downers Grove: IVP, 2000.

Feinberg, John. *No One Like Him*. Wheaton: Crossway Books, 2001.

Ferguson, Everett. *Backgrounds of Early Christianity*. Grand Rapids: Eerdmans, 2003.

Fox, Michael V. *Anchor Yale Bible: Proverbs 1-9*. New York: Doubleday, 2000.

Grudem, Wayne. *Systematic Theology*. Grand Rapids: Zondervan, 1994.

Hannah, Darrell D. *Michael and Christ: Michael Traditions and Angel Christology in Early Christianity*. Tübingen: Mohr Siebeck, 1999.

Harris, Elizabeth. *Prologue and Gospel: The Theology of the Fourth Evangelist*. JSNTSup 107. Sheffield: Sheffield Academic Press, 1995.

Harris, J. Rendel. *The Origin of the Prologue to St John's Gospel*. London: Cambridge University Press, 1917.

Harris, Murray J. *Jesus as God: The New Testament Use of Theos in Reference to Jesus*. Grand Rapids: Baker, 1992.

Hendriksen, William. *New Testament Commentary: John Volume 1*. Grand Rapids: Baker, 1953.

Holladay, William L. *A Concise Hebrew and Aramaic Lexicon of the Old Testament*. Grand Rapids: Eerdmans, 1971.

Hoskins, Paul M. *Jesus as the Fulfillment of the Temple in the Gospel of John*. Paternoster Biblical Monographs. Milton Keynes: Paternoster, 2006

Hurtado, Larry W. *How on Earth Did Jesus Become a God? Historical Questions About Earliest Devotion to Jesus*. Grand Rapids: Eerdmans, 2005.
———. *Lord Jesus Christ: Devotion to Jesus in Earliest Christianity*. Grand Rapids: Eerdmans, 2003.
———. "Does Philo Help Explain Early Christianity." In *Philo und das Neue Testament*, edited by Roland Deines and Karl-Wilhelm Niebuhr, 73-92. Tübingen: Mohr Siebeck, 2004.

Irons, Charles Lee. "A Lexical Defense Of The Johannine Only Begotten." In *Retrieving Eternal Generation*. Edited by Fred Sanders and Scott R. Swain, 98-116. Zondervan, 2017.

Kamesar, Adam. "The Logos Endiathetos and the Logos Prophorikos in Allegorical Interpretation: Philo and the D-Scholia to the Iliad." In *Greek, Roman and Byzantine Studies* 44 (2004): 163-81.

Keener, Craig S. *The Gospel of John: A Commentary*.
Peabody: Hendrickson Publishers, 2003.

Keil, Carl Friedrich. Delitzch, F. *Commentary on the Old
Testament in Ten Volumes*. Grand Rapids: Eerdmans,
1969.

Koehler, Ludwig, Walter Baumgartner, and M. E. J.
Richardon, eds. *The Hebrew and Aramaic Lexicon of
the Old Testament*. Accordance electronic ed., version
3.0. Leiden: Brill, 2000.

Koester, Craig R. *The Anchor Yale Bible: Revelation*. Yale,
2014.

Ladd, George Eldon. *A Theology of the New Testament*. Grand
Rapids: Eerdmans, 1993.

Lawson, George. *Exposition of the Book of Proverbs*.
Edinburgh: David Brown and W. Oliphant, 1821.

Lightfoot, R. H. St. *John's Gospel: A Commentary*. London:
Oxford University Press, 1956.

Longman, Tremper. *Proverbs*. Grand Rapids: Baker Academic,
2006.

Lust, Johan. Eynikel, Erik. Hauspie, Katrin. *Greek-English
Lexicon of the Septuagint*. Stuttgart: Deutsche
Bibelgesellschaft, 2003.

MacLeod, David J. "The Witness of John the Baptist to the
Word: John 1:6–9." In *Bibliotheca Sacra* (2003), 305–
20.

Mcdonough, Sean M. *Christ as Creator: Origins of a New
Testament Doctrine*. Oxford University Press, 2009.

Morris, Leon. *Studies in the Fourth Gospel*. Grand Rapids: Eerdmans, 1969.

Moule, C.F.D. *An Idiom Book of New Testament Greek*. Cambridge: Cambridge University Press, 1959.

Mueller, John Theodore. *Christian Dogmatics*. St Louis: Concordia Publishing House, 1934.

Murphy, Roland E. *The Tree of Life: An Exploration of Biblical Wisdom Literature*. Grand Rapids: Eerdmans, 1990.

Nash, Roland H. *The Gospel and the Greeks*. Phillipsburg: P&R Publishing, 2003.

Nestle, Erwin. Aland, Kurt. *Novum Testamentum Graece*. Stuttgart: Deutsche Bibelgesellschaft, 1993.

Nickelsburg, George W. E. "Philo among Greek, Jews and Christians." In *Philo und das Neue Testament*, edited by Roland Deines and Karl-Wilhelm Niebuhr, 53-72. Tübingen: Mohr Siebeck, 2004.

Oswalt, John N. *NICOT: The Book of Isaiah*. Eerdmans, 1998.

Pierce, Ronald Webster. *"Kanah" in Proverbs 8:22*. Talbot Theological Seminary, 1977.

Philo. *The Loeb Classical Library: Philo*. Edited by E. H. Warmington. 12 vols. Cambridge: Harvard University Press, 1930-1971.

Porter, Stanley E. *The Messiah in the Old and New Testaments*. Grand Rapids: Eerdmans, 2007.
————————. *Idioms of the Greek New Testament*. England: Sheffield Academic Press, 1999.

Rahlfs, Alfred. *Septuaginta*. Stuttgart: Deutsche
    Bibelgesellschaft, 1979.

Reim, Gunter "Jesus as God in the Fourth Gospel: The Old
    Testament Background." In *NTS* 30 (1984): 158–60

Ronning, John L. *The Jewish Targums and John's Logos
    Theology*. Peabody: Hendrickson Publishers, 2009

Runia, David T. *Philo of Alexandria and the Timaeus of Plato*.
    Leiden: E. J. Brill, 1986.
    ————————. "Philo of Alexandria." In *Routledge
    Encyclopedia of Philosophy*, edited by Edward Craig,
    357-361. New York: Routledge, 1998.
    ————————. *Philo in Early Christian Literature: A
    Survey*. Assen: Van Gorcum, 1993.

Schenck, Kenneth. *A Brief Guide to Philo*. Louisville: John
    Knox Press, 2005.

Schnackenburg, Rudolf. *The Gospel According to St. John*.
    New York: Herder & Herder, 1968.

Smalley, Stephen S. *John Evangelist & Interpreter*. Downers
    Grove: InterVarsity Press, 1998.

Sterling, Gregory E. "The Place of Philo of Alexandria in the
    Study of Christian Origins." In *Philo und das Neue
    Testament*, edited by Roland Deines and Karl-Wilhelm
    Niebuhr, 21-52. Tübingen: Mohr Siebeck, 2004.

Tobin, T.H. "The Prologue of John and Hellenistic Jewish
    Speculation." In *CBQ* 52 (1990): 252–69.

Toy, Crawford Howell. *A Critical and Exegetical Commentary
    on the Book of Proverbs*. New York: Scribner, 1899.

Turner, Nigel. Syntax. *Vol. 3 of A Grammar of New Testament Greek*, by J. H. Moulton. Edinburgh: T&T Clark, 1963.

Waetjen, Herman C. "Logos Pros Ton Theon and the Objectification of Truth in the Prologue of the Fourth Gospel." In *Catholic Biblical Quarterly* 63 (2001): 265-86.

Wahlde, Urban C. *The Gospel And Letters of John: Introduction, Analysis, and Reference*. Grand Rapids: Eerdmans, 2010.

Wallace, Daniel B. *Greek Grammar beyond the Basics*. Grand Rapids: Zondervan, 1996.

Waltke Bruce K. *NICOT: The Books of Proverbs Chapters 1-15*. Eerdmans, 2004.

Westcott, B. F. *The Gospel According to St. John: The Authorized Version with Introduction and Notes*. Grand Rapids: Eerdmans, 1971.

White, James R. *The Forgotten Trinity: Recovering the Heart of Christian Belief*. Minneapolis: Bethany House Publishers, 1998.

Whybray, R. N. *New Century Bible Commentary: Proverbs*. Grand Rapids: Eerdmans, 1994.

Winston, David. *The Wisdom of Solomon*. New York: Doubleday, 1979.

Witherington, Ben. *Jesus the Sage: The Pilgrimage of Wisdom*. Minneapolis: Fortress, 1994.

Wolfson, Harry Austryn. *Philo: Foundations of Religious Philosophy in Judaism, Christianity, and Islam*. Cambridge: Harvard University Press, 1962.

Index

1Clement
  25:2, 83
1Corinthians
  13:12, 35
1Irenaeus
  1:1, 83
1John, 34
  1:2, 34
2John
  1:2b, 35
3John
  1:4, 35
Aaron, 125
Abraham, 29, 71, 73, 79,
  80, 81, 82, 183
Accusative, 35, 46, 63, 93
Adam, 58, 133, 212
Aeon, 83
Agent of Creation, 53, 99,
  110, 114, 118, 140, 141,
  170, 179, 181, 185, 186,
  187, 204, 206
Agent of Revelation, 204,
  206
Aland, K., 214
Allegorization, 16, 135,
  136, 138
Amos

3:1,8, 200
Anaphoric, 39, 42
Anarthrous, 39, 40, 41, 42,
  44, 45, 108, 143, 144
Ancient, 30, 31, 110
Angel, 44, 54, 114, 128
Angel of the Lord, 11, 14,
  128, 129, 206
Aorist, 29
Apocryphal Gospels, 84
Aramaic, 195, 212
Archetype, 99, 100, 104,
  105, 106, 109, 113, 115,
  116, 130, 131, 132, 137
Architect, 110, 111, 181
Architecture, 105
Arians
  2:19, 84
  2:48, 84
  2:62, 85
  2:64, 86
  2:74, 86
  4:24, 87
  4:29, 87
Aristobolus
  4:3, 83
Aristotle, 145

Grudem, W., 47, 52, 54, 55,
211
Habakkuk
1:12, 31
Hagar, 127
HALOT, 74, 162, 168, 169,
170
Hannah, D.D., 104, 119,
120, 128, 129, 133, 145,
146, 211
Harris, E., 17, 133, 142,
191, 211
Harris, J.R., 152, 153, 176,
212
Harris, M.J., 17, 143, 144,
212
Heavens, 29, 50, 54, 170,
200, 201
Hebrew, 13, 25, 31, 46, 47,
67, 69, 72, 73, 78, 81, 89,
90, 108, 125, 151, 152,
157, 159, 160, 162, 165,
166, 167, 168, 169, 170,
199, 200, 201, 205, 209,
212
Hebrews
11:17, 71, 80
Heir, 74, 79, 85
Hellenism, 18, 22, 77, 101,
107, 133, 139, 181, 183,
184, 187, 190, 210, 215
Hendriksen, W., 14, 16,
212
High Priest, 123
Hippolytus, 84
Historical, 9, 20, 68, 105,
135, 136, 143, 144

History, 65, 107, 154
Holladay, W.L., 212
Hosea
1:7, 47
Hoskins, P.M., 13, 212
Human, 27, 53, 62, 68, 69,
105, 113, 115, 123, 124,
127, 131, 132, 135, 142,
166, 172, 176, 177, 178,
181, 184, 185, 186, 187,
191
Hurtado, L.W., 16, 17, 18,
133, 144, 191, 212
Hypostasis, 136, 184, 185,
187, 197
Identity, 42, 43, 44, 57, 84,
90
Image of an Image, 132
Immaterial, 109, 114, 132
Immortal, 116
Imperfective Aspect, 28, 29
Incarnation, 14, 22, 28, 36,
63, 68, 69, 76, 94, 95,
126, 127, 142, 172, 191,
205, 210
Incorporeal, 113
Infant, 170
Irenaeus, 83
Irons, C.L., 75, 76, 77, 79,
80, 81, 212
Isaac, 74, 79, 80, 81, 183
Isaiah, 14, 31, 46, 47, 51,
93, 95, 179, 205, 211,
214
1:3, 161
10:21, 69
2:5, 62